T0323703

Cambridge Elements ≡

Elements in Global Urban History
edited by
Michael Goebel
Graduate Institute Geneva
Tracy Neumann
Wayne State University
Joseph Ben Prestel
Freie Universität Berlin

OUR URBAN PLANET IN THEORY AND HISTORY

Carl H. Nightingale
University at Buffalo

CAMBRIDGE
UNIVERSITY PRESS

Shaftesbury Road, Cambridge CB2 8EA, United Kingdom

One Liberty Plaza, 20th Floor, New York, NY 10006, USA

477 Williamstown Road, Port Melbourne, VIC 3207, Australia

314–321, 3rd Floor, Plot 3, Splendor Forum, Jasola District Centre, New Delhi – 110025, India

103 Penang Road, #05–06/07, Visioncrest Commercial, Singapore 238467

Cambridge University Press is part of Cambridge University Press & Assessment, a department of the University of Cambridge.

We share the University's mission to contribute to society through the pursuit of education, learning and research at the highest international levels of excellence.

www.cambridge.org
Information on this title: www.cambridge.org/9781009494595

DOI: 10.1017/9781009321778

First published 2024

A catalogue record for this publication is available from the British Library.

ISBN 978-1-009-49459-5 Hardback
ISBN 978-1-009-32180-8 Paperback
ISSN 2632-3206 (online)
ISSN 2632-3192 (print)

Our Urban Planet in Theory and History

Elements in Global Urban History

DOI: 10.1017/9781009321778
First published online: May 2024

Carl H. Nightingale
University at Buffalo

Author for correspondence: Carl H. Nightingale, cn6@buffalo.edu

Abstract: This Element offers seven propositions toward a theory of "Our Urban Planet" that is useful to global urban historians. The author argues that historians have much to offer to theorists particularly those involved in debates over planetary urbanization theory and the Anthropocene. The concept of "urban" must be enlarged to include spaces that make cities possible and that cities make possible, allowing historians to operate on longer temporal frames, nesting global urban history within Earth Time. Above all, the crucial dimension of power needs to be added, redefining cities as spaces that humans produce to amplify harvests of geo-solar energy and deploy human power within space and time. This Element uses insights from "deep history" to set the stage for a "theory by verb" elaborating the many paradoxes of humans' 6,000-year gamble with the Urban Condition and explaining cities' own intrinsic capacity to outrun their own theorizability.

This Element also has a video abstract: www.cambridge.org/EGUB-Carl

Keywords: planetary urbanization, global urban history, urban theory, Anthropocene, urban studies

ISBNs: 9781009494595 (HB), 9781009321808 (PB), 9781009321778 (OC)
ISSNs: 2632-3206 (online), 2632-3192 (print)

Contents

The foundation of cities … is … the most important material prerequisite for power.

     — Hanna Arendt, *The Human Condition* ([1958] 2018, 201)

In principle urban historians have the opportunity to become the most important interpreters of the ways that global social processes articulate with small-scale social life. No use talking about it; someone will have to do it!

     — Charles Tilly, "What Good Is Urban History?" (1996, 702)

At stake is a critical urban theory attentive to historical difference as a fundamental constituting process of global political economy.

     — Ananya Roy, "What is Critical about Critical Urban Theory?" (2015, 1)

Planetary urbanization is a historical and not a universal phenomenon.

     — Christian Schmid, "Journeys in Planetary Urbanization" (2018, 592)

Where is the Theory in Urban History?

     — Richard Harris, *How Cities Matter* (2021, 8)

Today, as the power centers of a truly planetary Urban Planet, cities place our own unequal communities in precarious command of Earth's fertile lithosphere, its watery hydrosphere, it Sun-moderating atmosphere, and the entirety of its profuse halo of life.

     — Carl H. Nightingale, *Earthopolis: A Biography of Our Urban Planet* (2022, 1)

The city took everything into its clutches and sent it every which way. Maybe you had a say in which direction, and maybe you didn't.

     — Colson Whitehead, *Harlem Shuffle* (2021, 146)

Preliminary Matters I: Space, Time, and Power

In this Element, I sketch out seven propositions for a historical theory of Our Urban Planet. The history that supports the theory comes from my experience of writing a synthesis of historical and archeological research from across the 6,000-year lifespan of global urban history. My main goal is to offer framing insight – theory – that is useful to global urban historians as researchers, interpreters of change, teachers, and students. I also hope that a historical theory of "Our Urban Planet" is useful to professional theorists involved in debates over "planetary urbanization" and the "Anthropocene" – especially since many of these scholars have appealed to "history" as a solution to limitations of theory.

My propositions weave history with theory upon a conceptual grid with three axes, each calibrated in scope from very small to very large: *space* on the *x*-axis; *time* on the *y*-axis; and, most importantly, *power* on the *z*-axis.

Space. Cities and Our Urban Planet are spaces made up of many others that can take many nested and overlapping sizes, shapes, and scopes, all of them with blurry boundaries. I propose expanding the spatial scope of the urban, and thus of global urban history and urban theory, to include non-city spaces that *made cities possible* – urban hinterlands – and spaces that *cities made possible* – which I call "urban forelands." Non-cities in these urban hinterlands and forelands partake of "the urban" to varying degrees and encompass spaces that we can additionally, and with equal usefulness, classify as rural, extractive, or infrastructural. Urban hinterlands and forelands can also include parts or all of Earth's extra-human biological ecosystems and geophysical spaces ultimately created and governed by the Sun. Urban spaces that are specifically designed by humans take a variety of forms, and today's theorists are right to notice that these forms blur into each other, as they always have, to a varied extent. Even today, though, as these urban spaces accelerate in size, the urban can still be usefully divided into *relatively thick* spaces (large and concentrated cities themselves, including their blurry peripheries), *relatively thin* spaces (even larger but dispersed rural and "natural" city-producing and city-produced spaces), and *relatively threadlike* spaces (typically called infrastructures, also larger in scale than cities, and distinguished, like thread, by their elongated and interconnective form).

In my propositions, I sum up these overlapping urban spaces – city + hinterland + foreland, and their thick + thin + threadlike spatial skeleton – as "the Urban Condition," a specific spatially determined manifestation of the human condition that first arose when we began building cities. When component spaces of the Urban Condition achieve planetary dimensions, historians may enter one of many birthdays of Our Urban Planet into the registers of time. Still, note that in defining the Urban Condition and Our Urban Planet this way – again, as city-producing and city-produced space – my theory of the urban retains its foundation on the existence and historical importance of cities.

As spaces, cities, the Urban Condition, and Our Urban Planet are *singularities* in two senses of that word. They are unique in the universe, as far as we now know. They also share important historical attributes consistently across space and time – everywhere and always – that I will explore in depth in my propositions. However, from their varied birth in time and space, cities, the Urban Condition, and the Urban Planet have always been, for practical purposes, almost infinitely plural. In that paradox of plural singularity, urban spaces mirror the human species, even as, over time, the human condition itself became increasingly defined by the Urban Condition and the habitation of Our Urban Planet.

Time. Cities, the Urban Condition, and Our Urban Planet exist *in time* paradoxically as durable yet changeable as well as variable historical phenomena. It is useful to appreciate the history of urban spaces in both very short and very long temporal contexts. My propositions focus on long time, framing the 6,000 years of global urban history within the 300,000 years of "deep" human history and amongst the most recent epochal shifts in the 4.5 billion years of planetary history as measured by the Geological Time Scale.

Cities are also spaces where we bend time. We design them to allow us to produce simultaneous and polyrhythmic changes in time of many sizes and shapes, including continuities, self-propelling processes, disruptions, "resurfacings," "hauntings," "entanglements," and many unforeseeable contingencies and "miracles" (Arendt, 1958; Gordon, 2008; Stoler, 2016). This is true because the temporal dimensions of cities and the Urban Condition are governed by the foundational – one might say ontological – relationship between our production of space and our production of human power.

Power. Cities, the Urban Condition, and Our Urban Planet are the historical products and producers of two forms of *power*. The first encompasses all manifestations of geophysical energy delivered by the Sun and Earth – the sources of all air, water, food, warmth, fuel, building materials, and thus all human and extra-human life energy. The second form encompasses all power deployed through individual and collective projects of human action, institutionalized or otherwise. These two forms of power, which I will distinguish as *geo-solar energy* and *human power*, are made in space and time. They also *make* space and time. At specific historical moments, cities became the preeminent spatial vehicles for the enlargement and concentration of human harvests of geo-solar energy – and from that, the production of human power both over other humans and over other extra-human life-forms and spaces. Cities' centrality to the Urban Condition in space, and their capacity to bend time, rests above all on the relation of thick space to power and are best defined by three categories of action involved in deriving human power from human space: To Produce, that is all acts necessary to create human space and power; To Amplify, all acts required to create "thicker" space and the power we can wield in it; and To Deploy, acts involved in wielding thickened space and power. All three of these broad categories of action consist of multiple subcomponents which I explore in Propositions 3 and 4.

Cities allowed humans to act collectively on larger spatial scales by means of "projects" of power production, amplification, deployment, and their many components and the purposes for them, typically enabled by institutions, movements, or other large-scale collective practices that were less possible when we only lived in smaller, thinner spaces. Since cities came into being 6,000 years ago, they therefore played a necessary, if always insufficient, role in any interpretation of our species' capacity to alter space and time – in both small and very large increments, in diverse ways, often including very inequitable ways. It follows that cities themselves are critical causal agents in human history.

To usefully explain change, a historical theory of Our Urban Planet must imagine space, time, and power as operating in dialectical relationships governed by the rule that each component is *necessary but insufficient* to explain the other. The causes of change in urban history always take the form of multiple intersecting dialectical relationships between cities and a wide range of space-, time-, and power-producing projects of many sizes and scopes that include human acts of all kinds, and the interactions of these projects with extra-human life-forms and geophysical forces. By examining the many intersecting dialectics that result, a history-inflected theory can supply useful insight to our discussions of vexed concepts like cities, the Urban, and Our Urban Planet. However, the sheer volatility of projects of production, amplification, and deployment of urban-based human power in history explains why cities and the Urban will always defy any full, universal, or even "total" definitions; why diversity, inequality, and unpredictability will always lie at their heart; why their spatial components have always had blurry boundaries; and, from there, also why these foundationally historical phenomena will always remain partly beyond reach of theory alone.

Preliminary Matters II: Global Urban History, "Planetary Urbanization," and the "Anthropocene"

The seven propositions about Our Urban Planet that I offer here took shape in response to three contemporaneous, but largely separate scholarly debates. All three grew in energy and scope during the 2010s, and all show signs of inflecting each other in the 2020s. The first consists of conversations among urban historians about the usefulness of urban theory for our work on the urban past, notably as a guide for the field's expanding interest in questions of global and planetary dimensions. The second is the much louder debate in urban theory itself over the concept "planetary urbanization." The third is the equally vociferous multidisciplinary debate – spanning the Earth Systems Sciences, the social sciences, and the humanities – over the movement in the field of geology to use the term "Anthropocene" to designate a new Epoch in the Geological Time Scale, defined above all by "human activities" and the resulting existential predicaments that define our own time.

Theory of, for, and by Urban Historians. During the 2010s, growing numbers of urban historians grew restless for a body of urban theory of our own. The sentiment, which has earlier precedents (see Harris, 2021, 8–14), derives in part from a complaint that professional urban theorists rarely reference our field's massive body of collective work. But it also arises from within, for we rarely take time to intervene in theoretical debates ourselves, nor to produce theory of our own in print. As a result, we possess no body of theoretical work that responds to our specific needs as primary researchers largely in archives; that reflects our general tendency to favor multicausal and multidirectional arguments capable of explaining continuities, disruptions, contingencies, and other forms of change over time, including the *longue durée* of urban history; that helps guide larger scale spatiotemporal narratives germane to the cities we work on; and that speaks a language that is directly tailored for students of urban history.

This theoretical restlessness has found a few outlets – in well-attended panels at our conferences that take up old foundational questions like "what is a city," and in an extended essay by the historical geographer Richard Harris entitled *Why Cities Matter* (Harris, 2021). The quest for theoretical insight also found a venue in the Global Urban History Project (GUHP), founded in 2017 to build a home for urban historians working on cities across the world including in regions underrepresented in the field, and to promote the study of "cities as the creations and creators of larger-scale and even global phenomena" (GUHP, 2020). A committee of GUHP scholars has since devoted one of the association's "Dream Conversations" to the subject "Urban Theory of, for, and by Urban Historians." In its statement of purpose, the committee, of which I am a member, complains that "urban historians are importers of theory, rarely producers or exporters" and asks,

> what would happen if urban historians took an inventory of our theoretical vocabulary, checked its archaeology, reassessed its usefulness, exposed its blind spots, rediscovered alternatives we overlooked – especially from scholarship in the Global South? Should we recalibrate the proportion of concepts from different sources, search elsewhere for useful theory, ask what we might do without theory, or even generate concepts of our own more useful to us as primary researchers? (GUHP, 2021)

My work has focused on elaborating the idea that cities are "creators of larger scale phenomena." To do that, I believe, urban historians need to go beyond our expertise in narratives of space and time and to theorize cities in terms of power, and thus as causal agents in world history. This was the mission of my book *Earthopolis* (*EP*; Nightingale 2022). The book's three parts identify the principal non-city gathering grounds and conduits of geo-solar energy necessary for cities and deployments of urban power: rivers, for the first 5,500 years of global urban history; the World Ocean from 1500 to about 1780 CE; and deposits of hydrocarbon fuels from 1780 CE to the present. In its twenty-five chapters, the book describes cities' dialectical relationships with the most powerful human activities in world history: states, empires, social movements, wealth-accumulating enterprises, knowledge-making and knowledge-disseminating institutions, and expansions or contractions in human mobility and reproduction. Along the way, *Earthopolis* documents the growth and retreat in space and time of the power that humans deployed from cities. I classified these spaces as Realms of Action, Realms of Habitat, Realms of Impact, and Realms of Consequence. In this Element, I designate these types of space "urban forelands." Like urban hinterlands, urban forelands accelerated to planetary scope at different times, notably after 1500, after 1780, and during the "Greatest Acceleration" from 1945 to the present (*EP*, 1–14). Note that *Earthopolis* is primarily a work of global urban history, not a work of theory. However, the task of writing it nurtured the tendrils of all seven propositions I will make in this essay.

Planetary Urbanization. The second body of scholarly work I address in these propositions is the debate on the theory of "planetary urbanization" – derived from neo-Marxist writings of the urban theorist Henri Lefebvre, and most closely associated with the recent work of the theorist Neil Brenner and the geographer Christian Schmid. Debates over this concept grew in energy and fury during the late 2010s, drawing in many prominent scholars in the fields of critical urban theory, geography, postcolonial theory, feminist and queer theory, and urban political ecology. Brenner and Schmid have elaborated their ideas in response to their critics, but the concept has remained deeply controversial, as most vividly attested by contributions to a 2018 special issue of the journal *Environment and Planning B*. My seven propositions obliquely respond to the seven "theses" Brenner and Schmid proposed early in this debate (2015), and that they have largely defended ever since. Meanwhile, scholars in the small field of urban political ecology took a theoretical tack that resembles mine in some respects (e.g. Kaika et al., 2023), by interrogating the role of the "extended" urban in the predicaments of the Anthropocene. The work of critics of planetary urbanization also helps guide some of my propositions here.

For global urban historians, the most useful and challenging of Brenner and Schmid's theses pertains to space: namely, their central argument that "urbanization has become planetary" (Brenner and Schmid 2015, 172). The idea that, as Brenner later put it, the urban occupies "planetary space as a whole, including not only the terrestrial surfaces, but the underground, the oceans, and even the atmosphere itself" (Brenner 2017, 36) is intrinsically linked to a broader point that "the urban" cannot be limited to cities alone. I agree that historians can learn much from thinking harder about the "mutually constitutive" relationship between what Brenner and Schmid call "concentrated urbanization" (cities) and spaces encompassed by what they call "extended urbanization." I also agree strongly with them when they urge us to think hard about "the relentless 'churning' of urban configurations at all spatial scales" (Brenner and Schmid 2015, 165), approximating what I and other historians have called "diascalar" or "transpatial" dynamics (Nightingale 2015; Schayegh 2017). In response to early critiques that "planetary urbanization" emphasized homogeneity or even "totality" over difference, Brenner and Schmid's (2015) manifesto also elaborated the concept of "differentiated urbanization." As such, they explored the diversity, inequality, and "uneven development" encompassed by concentrated and extended urbanization more than their critics sometimes acknowledge. Indeed, planetary urbanization theory was always embedded in a larger theory of capitalist inequality.

That said, Brenner and Schmid's insistence on calling planetary urbanization a "historical totality" does raise questions about the relationship between very large phenomena and their smaller-scale creators and creations that are central to all the propositions in this Element. These questions also lay at the heart of the firestorm of critique that greeted planetary urbanization theory, for the spatial scope of inquiry has become something of an indicator of political affiliation within the field of critical theory. As neo-Marxists "go big," postcolonial, feminist, and queer theorists often favor smaller-bore, "situated" epistemologies. My field, *global urban* history, straddles this divide more comfortably: Most of us are just as willing to accept Anaya Roy and Aihwa Ong's idea of "worlding practices" (e.g. Ong, 2012) – large-scale phenomena with many smaller-scale origins – as we are to accept the opposite, that all smaller things emerge in larger contexts. The propositions that follow, accordingly, rest on a paradox of "plural singularity" and treat it as the product of dialectical interchanges between multiple larger generalities and smaller specificities. That dialectic, in turn, makes up one of many other mutually constituting relationships of power between humanity, cities, the urban, and the planetary in space and time.

The large scope of Brenner and Schmid's theory of space is less of a problem for historians than their more specific insistence on superseding what Hillary Angelo and David Wachsmuth call "methodological city-ism" (Angelo and Wachsmuth, 2014). Because urbanization cannot be equated with cities alone, they argue, urban theory must set aside its central reliance on the category *city*. I disagree. Historians – least of all global urban ones – should not backpedal even slightly on the historical importance of cities themselves, least of all to deepen our understanding of things like "extended urbanism" or "differentiated urbanization." When Brenner and Schmid originally advertised planetary urbanization as a theory of "urbanization without an outside," they also effectively deprioritized theoretical distinctions between cities and what I think we ought to call non-cities. Indeed, their chief early critic, Ananya Roy, rightly pressed them to account for ongoing and very real differences between cities – which she and other critics continued to, at least ambiguously, equate with the "urban" as a whole – and rural, infrastructural, and natural spaces (Roy, 2015).

What is missing in both Brenner and Schmid's analysis and Roy's response is a theory flexible enough to recognize cities as central to the urban – and thus requiring ongoing theorization in their own right – but that simultaneously recognizes that the category urban can exist as a graduated adjective that encompasses non-cities, while also allowing us to theorize non-cities' very real differences with cities. Brenner and Schmid's concepts "extended urbanization" and "differentiated urbanization" gesture in this direction, but they are too blunt and sweeping, a problem I propose to resolve through the spatiotemporal taxonomies of "the Urban" divided into subcategories of cities and noncities; of thick, thin, threadlike spaces; and of various types of urban hinterlands and urban forelands. As my opening epigraphs to this essay imply, Brenner, Schmid, Roy, and other urban theorists often express the idea that "the historical" matters to basic questions of urban theory. I, of course, agree. However, erasing "methodological city-ism" unnecessarily throws out a very useful path toward a historical theory of the city that builds on ideas proposed by Henri Lefebvre himself, notably that cities and the urban consist in part of "practices" (Lefebvre, 1970 [2003], 1974 [1991]). My propositions elaborate this point by identifying what I believe to be the three essential types of action – To Produce, To Amplify, and To Deploy – required for a definition of cities as pivot points in historical dialectics of space, time, and power – as well as between phenomena that range from very large to very small.

Indeed, if planetary urbanization theorists' conceptions of space are only partly useful to historians, the same is true of their treatment of urban spatial power. Brenner and Schmid's demotion of cities' theoretical importance serves to elevate a single form of urban amplified power, what they call "processes of capitalist urbanization," to central, even quasi-monocausal status. In their hands, planetary urbanization is approximately equivalent to capitalist urbanization operating at a planetary scale – a phenomenon they go so far as to call a "historical totality."[1] Undeniably, this theoretical move has at least some use for historians, since the historical record repeatedly confirms the sheer

---

[1] In a more recent online multimedia project, Schmid and his colleagues at the ETH Zürich (Future Cities Laboratory, 2023) appear to have backed off somewhat on this position. Much of their empirical exploration of "extreme territories of urbanization" consists of mapping of very large urban hinterlands required to make twenty-first-century cities operate. In the explicatory text, "urbanization" appears to refer to the creation of sourcing grounds needed for cities, not the needs of capitalists, though of course these needs overlap extensively. In that way, the authors more closely approximate arguments I make in Proposition 2.

importance of the accumulation of wealth and capital to the shape of cities as well as that of bigger spaces that I call urban hinterlands and forelands. Also useful is Brenner and Schmid's understanding that capital accumulation is highly prone to crises that demand what the geographer David Harvey elegantly called "spatial fixes" (Harvey, 1989). Their vision of capitalist urbanization is correctly complex, involving dialectics of crisis and fix, and of creation and destruction. In history, urban spatial production and wealth accumulation have always been intertwined, and the accumulation of wealth designated "capital" became increasingly intertwined with the production of urban space over time. Today, capitalist practices are essential to understanding the birth of Our Urban Planet and the predicaments that define Our Time. As such, global urban historians must treat capitalism in its many forms as a crucial instrument in the deployment of urban-amplified human power, engaged in necessary-yet-insufficient dialectical relationships with cities and other urban spaces as both a crucial producer and a crucial product.

The problem is the "totality" of the argument as a causal interpretation and thus as a theory of human power and city-amplified human power specifically. As Brenner and Schmid's critics point out, and as they are aware themselves, even in our own time of advanced capitalism, capitalist urbanization affects the cities of the world in highly unequal or "uneven" ways, most glaringly in the form of inequalities and differences between (and within) the Global North and the Global South. It is plausible, therefore, to critique theories that identify capitalism as the primary – let alone the only – force of urbanization as demoting the sheer impact of five hundred years of state action, colonization, slavery, labor exploitation, imperialism, racism, and anti-nature beliefs, all infused by patriarchal gender ideologies. In that way, neo-Marxist theories also expose themselves to the charge of Eurocentrism.

These shortcomings of their theory of power are compounded by limitations in their conception of time. Modern-era capital accumulation, even when understood in the context of other early-modern and modern forces, is only one of many formidable, crisis-prone, "spatial-fix"-seeking forces with which global urban historians need to grapple. Other instruments of human power that have similarly dialectical relationships to cities – and to the urban more generally – include: ancient temple cliques, city-states, kingdoms, empires, nation-states, the great "Axial Age" religions, much emerging evidence of premodern social movements, modern social movements and revolutions, modern secular ideologies, global consumer culture, the complexities of architectural, public health, and urban planning discourses, many major technological revolutions, millennia of demographic expansions and contractions, mass migrations, and environmental change. In addition, we must contend with many forms of premodern and modern wealth accumulation (and crises and fixes thereof) whose specific relationship to "capital" is a highly vexed matter, chewed on in many ways in separate subfields that cover many periods and geographical spaces. Finally, there is also the substantial matter of "anti-capitalist" urbanization. By training, urban historians – even those of us inclined to prioritize capitalism as a central causal force – are correctly sensitive to the complex interplay of causalities. The monocausal bent of planetary urbanization theory makes it less useful for that endeavor.

Planetary urbanization theory's lack of chronology, beyond a hazily defined recent past, reconfirms a basic reason for historians' mistrust of theorists more generally. In the propositions that follow, I seek to remedy that matter. First, this historical theory rests on a chronological analysis of all 6,000 years of global urban history that traces many forms of energy concentration and power deployment including capitalism. Second, I reject Brenner and Schmid's implication that extended and differentiated urban space is somehow a novel historical phenomenon. And thirdly, I dig deeper into the relationship of cities and time by interrogating the temporal concept "process" itself – which historians have borrowed profusely and uncritically from theorists – and recommending the idea of "project" as the primary basis for an exploration of the "polyrhythmic" nature of urban temporality (Proposition 6).

The Anthropocene. The third intellectual development that overlapped with my effort to write a biography of "Our Urban Planet" was a dramatic expansion of the scholarly debate on the concept "Anthropocene."

Spatially, the "Planet Earth" of the Anthropocene debate is only scantly concerned with concepts from planetary urbanization theory like "extended" and "differentiated urbanization," though urban political ecologists have begun to make this connection (e.g. Tzaninis et al., 2023). Earth Systems scientists typically treat "cities" as discrete from other spaces, though they recognize that the carbon footprint of buildings, industry, and transport systems in cities has a much larger reach. Some have usefully estimated the weight of the entire human-built environment (Elhacham et al., 2020); others the percentage of Earth's surface covered by the "anthrome," the sum of all human-built or human-altered spaces (Elis and Ramankutty, 2008); and still others the size of the "technosphere," the space occupied by everything humans have made, including all built structures plus all human things that are, strictly speaking, not part of the built environment (Haff, 2014). But "the planet" natural scientists have in mind involves far more: the transformations of the biological, chemical, physical, and caloric composition of virtually all solid, liquid, and gaseous components of Earth's surface, its immediate subsurface, and near-space; radical alterations and displacements of many of Earth's biological ecosystems;

transformed geochemical and geophysical systems such as the carbon, nitrogen, and phosphorus cycles; alterations in the direction of ocean currents; and even changes in the location of Earth's magnetic poles and the tilt of Earth's axis. Thanks to exploding volumes of human-generated greenhouse gas, the space affected by the predicaments of the Anthropocene encompasses changes in Earth's energy-regulating and life-ensuring relationship to the Sun. Geologists note that all such phenomena leave immense indelible traces in the fossil record, meaning that they not only imprint space on a planetary scale, but all future Earth Time (Thomas et al., 2020).

Indeed, the sense of time that governs the Anthropocene debate is also far more extensive than that encompassed by planetary urbanization, let alone by global urban history. At issue is the proposal to add the "Anthropocene" as the 38th Epoch in the 4.5 billion-year Geological Time Scale, with the goal of distinguishing the present time on Earth as uniquely "Ours." Under the original proposal – adopted widely within and outside the natural sciences despite its rejection by a subcommission of professional geologists – the advent of the new epoch would signal the end of its predecessor, the Holocene Epoch, after a mere 11,700 years. The new threshold would additionally suggest that "Earth Time" has accelerated dramatically in relation to the rhythm of previous epochal transitions, which bookended periods measured in millions, not thousands, of years. Finally, it would divide human time into three distinct geological periods, starting with our "deep" origins 300,000 years ago during the earlier Pleistocene Epoch, followed by the period of our vast expansion during the Holocene, and the period of existential tumult we could face in the newest, likely much hotter, Epoch to come.

That said, smaller increments of time are also at stake in this debate, and a finer-grained periodization of the epochal transition remains very much up for grabs, if not completely unformed. Under conventions established by the International Union of Geological Scientists, the "zero hour" of new epochs must be distinguished from earlier ones by a "Golden Spike" in the stratigraphic record. They settled on deposits of anthropogenic plutonium and other materials in a Canadian lake-bottom dating from 1950 (Thomas, 2022). That moment rhymes closely with the beginning of the "Great Acceleration" in the Urban Condition, and it closely parallels other "J-curve" or "hockey-stick" accelerations in other human acts and impacts on the planet. Pounding a Golden Spike into 1950 CE, however, leaves open questions about the obvious precursors of those deposits, such as the industrial revolution and the rise in greenhouse gas wastes that have since tipped Earth into a heating pattern uncharacteristic of the Holocene. Others have rightly pointed to the rise of global capitalism, Atlantic slavery, imperialism, racism, and the simultaneous rise of particularly destructive and exploitative human views of nature. For them, the "Capitalocene," "Racial Capitalocene," or even "Plantationocene" would be better names for the predicaments we face today. These critics push the beginning of any new Epoch by as much as 500 years, to the expansions of European power dating to the early modern period (e.g. Moore, 2017; Vergès, 2017). Questions also remain about humans' longer interactions with Earth Time. Most of humanity's experience on Earth occurred under the Pleistocene Epoch's highly volatile temperature shifts, with severe "Ice Ages" alternating with warmer "interglacial" periods. The onset of far-less volatile "Goldilocks" energy fluctuations during the Holocene is widely credited for enabling humans to experiment with agriculture – and six millennia after that, with cities. Nonetheless, the irregular temporal rhythms of the Holocene continued to be important to human activities, possibly helping to explain periods of expansion and collapse in the space occupied by the Urban Condition. Conversely, human land use practices and emissions from city-feeding agriculture may have helped to stabilize Holocenic patterns somewhat as well, long before we radically disrupted those patterns, largely by burning hydrocarbon fuels on a massive scale (Zalasiewicz and Williams, 2012; Ruddiman 2014; Brooke, 2014).

To critics of the Anthropocene project from the humanities and social sciences, questions of space and time are less important than questions of power. To them, the idea, as one pair of Earth Systems scientists has put it, that something as large as an epochal transition was caused by the "geological superpower" of "human activities" (Lewis and Maslin, 2018) seems far too vague and undifferentiated. By ignoring inequalities of power, critics conclude, "Anthropocene" risks falsely accusing billions of humans who contribute very little to the many predicaments we face today, and who suffer the most from them, of being equal perpetrators of eco-atrocity – while also erasing stories of Holocene-friendly practices they have engaged in, sometimes for millennia. Many of these critics emphasize that a causal theory resting on *anthropos* risks exonerating the true villains of the story. Thus far, the alternative names they propose, such as Capitalocene and Plantationocene, have largely escaped the accusation, repeatedly faced by planetary urbanization theorists, that explanations for Earth-wide dynamics that center capitalism or even racial capitalism risk "totality" themselves. Other critics turn upon the credibility of Earth Systems Science as a field, noting that geologists in particular have long deployed their knowledge in service of coal, gas, and oil extraction – or faulting scientists' positivist epistemologies as anti-democratic, expert-driven forms of knowledge production that represent another form of totality (e.g. Yusoff, 2019). Nonetheless, most Anthropocene critics affirm the reality of the multiple predicaments we face as a species and as inhabitants of a highly destabilized planet. Thus, they share a foundational political bond with Anthropocene-advocates in opposing forms of propaganda such as "climate denialism," that have sunk deep into popular culture worldwide even as scholars battled internally over relatively esoteric proposals regarding Earth Time.

Preliminary Matters III: The "Our" in "Our Urban Planet"

The propositions that follow offer global urban historians seven pathways toward a historical theory of Our Urban Planet that build on the most useful parts of planetary urbanization theory and the Anthropocene project, while also tapping the critiques of totality that arose in debates about both. My propositions stress the usefulness of highly calibrated, blurry, yet still city-centered taxonomies of urban space, time, and power, layering these from the outset upon the compound paradoxes that arise from conceiving humanity as a plural singularity. As such, I hope my proposals multiply the possibilities for global urban historical narratives that emphasize the many highly differentiated and unequal ways our species has used space and power to interact with the energies of the Sun and Earth in past time – while keeping our interpretative lenses wide open to enormities like the existential predicaments we all face in the present and future. Indeed, if the history and theory I offer has an epistemological bottom line, it is that Our Time has robbed us of the luxury of privileging big or small; long or short; general or specific; singular or plural; Urban or Planetary (compare Chakrabarty, 2021).

In that vein, I deliberately highlight the "Our" in "Our Urban Planet." I do that in full awareness of the risks, for it is true that the greatest Earth-destroyers of our time have specialized in colonizing the first-person-plural pronoun as a means to normalize their depredations and their ill-meaning denialist ideologies. I believe, however, that We/Us/Our remains too indispensable a conceptual space to write off. The colonization of any pronoun anywhere demands its decolonization and recapture everywhere, not any wholesale surrender to ill-meaning propaganda mills – let alone to the well-meaning but ultimately defeatist idea that "We" must inevitably absolve arch-villains, validate Eurocentric positions, or advance positivism or totality. Recall this: Among the pronouns, only first-person-plural intrinsically invokes plurality and singularity, and diversity and similarity. It alone embraces both sides of humanity's undeniably paradoxical existence as a multifariously embodied yet intrinsically embedded species. To be truly useful, a historical theory of the urban must contribute, not to burying "We," but – as environmental justice activists usefully remind us – to building "Bigger We's" to come (e.g. Climate Justice Alliance, 2020).

Proposition 1: Start Deep Not Total – Humans, Space, and Power

Tentative explorations of *deep history* offer useful alternatives to theoretical *totality* for interpretations of large, plural-yet-singular phenomena like the human, the city, the urban, the global, and the planetary. By contemplating humanity from our deep historical origins some 300,000 years ago, these perspectives allow us to (1) explore the roots of these plural singularities alongside their other paradoxical features, (2) explore the limits of both universalizing and differentiating epistemologies, and (3) treat dialectical interchanges between relatively large and relatively small phenomena as crucial dynamics in human history that apply usefully to global urban history and to a historical theory of Our Urban Planet.

Historians – urban historians, perhaps exceptionally so – are trained to be allergic to "totality." Putting aside the complicity of totality in top-down, one-size-fits-all visions of perfect cities (Proposition 7), it can also stand in for epistemological indifference to human diversity or inequality, simplistic mono-causality, temporal unidirectionality, the mechanization of change, teleology, and unquestioned universality – all of which most historians learn early in our training to avoid. The fact that totality figures so strongly in the work of "planetary urbanization" theorists and has become the major focus of the theory's critics should give historians pause about any usefulness of concepts like "Our Urban Planet" for historical research – let alone as a pathway into another "total"-seeming concept, the "Anthropocene."

Can we talk about big things without slouching toward totality? Some critical theorists and historians have foresworn large concepts altogether for analyses that are "situated" – for example, in the lived experience of workers, the enslaved, colonized subjects, women, and LGBTQ+ people – and that privilege the agency they bring to experiences of repression and erasure, notably at the hands of those whose overweening power benefits from invidious totalistic claims. Others, like Ananya Roy and Aihwa Ong, have argued that such diverse, situated, or subaltern agencies provide the best route to understanding phenomena that operate on larger scales (Ong, 2012; Roy 2015). Still another way of handling the problem of totality is that proposed by the theorist Kanishka Goonewarneda in his highly learned contribution to the contentious 2018 issue of *Planning and Environment D* on planetary urbanization. He notes that the vast canon of neo-Marxist, feminist, postcolonial, and urban critical theory, including that of Henri Lefebvre, contains many more flexible conceptions of totality, including "dialectical notions of contradiction, difference, mediation, and articulation ... most helpful to theorize how capitalism, patriarchy, and colonialism co-determine the complex whole of society" (Goonewardena, 2018, 467). Goonewardena's concept of totality provides a useful basis for multicausal, multidirectional, and polyrhythmic theories of the global and planetary urban. It also resonates well with the multicausal analyses of the roles of slavery, settler colonialism, and racial capitalism underlying concepts like the Plantationocene. It also more closely corresponds to the call by Yannis Tzaninis and other urban political ecologists to explore the intersections of all forces of historic injustice with "more-than-human" transformations (Tzaninis et al., 2023, 3–6).

As historians, it is useful to note two things about these remedies for totality. Temporally, they start in the present and wander backward into ever-blurrier chronologies of modern and early modern eras. Epistemologically, their thrust is generally toward increased differentiation and complication, generally privileging plurality over singularity. Yet as critical theorists with solid anti-racist credentials know well, shortchanging (let alone denying) shared attributes of humanity can be as politically perilous as erasing diversity. To the extent that any shared attributes matter to cities, the urban, the global urban, or the planetary urban – all of them quintessential products of human action, no matter how diverse or unequal – we should be willing to allow singularity to share theoretical space with plurality.

"Deep history" represents another fruitful alternative to totality. It is a tiny, highly speculative subfield, and it could be easy, amidst the scream of today's existential predicaments, to dismiss its claims about humans during the earliest periods of our 300,000-year existence on Earth. Its practitioners' archive is a secondary one, mostly consisting of the published work of paleontologists, paleoanthropologists, and paleogeneticists whose research epistemologies can smell of lingering positivism, even as they produce highly uncertain results. That said, deep historians' method is compelling: They train a humanist's eye on this scientific archive of 99.8 percent of the human experience to identify "patterns, frames, metaphors" (Shryock and Smail 2011, xi) that "shallower" historians overlook – as do even-more myopic theorists – either because we demote them as mere "prehistory," or maybe because they hide in such plain sight.

One insight that jumps out concerns the relationship between the production of human space, human power, our actions in time, and a home planet and a star whose energies sumptuously produce life yet can just as easily snatch life away. Nested within that paradoxical context of life-giving and life-taking energy lies a second one, if my somewhat abstracted version[2] of deep history is correct:

---

[2] Legal theorists will note that I also draw upon Martha Albertson Fineman's "vulnerability theory" for this reading (e.g. Fineman, 2024).

namely that we possess a unique range of both powers and vulnerabilities. That second paradox nests within a third, for both our power and our vulnerability arise amidst co-creating existential states of embodiment (we exist only in bodies) and embeddedness (we *interact*, therefore we exist). It follows that our existence depends on gambling that we can deploy the power that the Sun and Earth give to our distinctively designed body forms and our distinctively large and effective, if highly vexed, social networks, in ways that minimize the vulnerabilities of our bodies and societies to bursts of geo-solar energy of many types that threaten us with death. In my reading, deep historical narratives turn on basic actions – or "practices" – required to take this gamble: verbs such as to reproduce, to care, to think, to communicate, to move, to labor, to innovate, to forage, to harvest, to accumulate, to ritualize, to institutionalize governance solutions for tensions inherent to our embodied embeddedness, and to narrate legitimating and critical stories about those institutions. Among these nests another practice that resonates especially deeply throughout the 6,000 "shallower" years of global urban history: namely *to produce our space* – above all to produce shelter, a narrative the paleoanthropologist Jerry D. Moore calls the "prehistory of home" (Moore, 2012).

Accepting any of these deep actions and the "narrative motifs" (Shryock and Smail, 2011, x) they set in motion as emblems of a shared "human condition" is a far cry from any totalistic epistemology. Whether deep historians have these narratives exactly right or not, it is easy to see how each of these stories of existence-sustaining human action can be enacted in nearly infinite ways and, from there, reconstructed in a further infinity of different ways using humans' vast powers of institutional invention, extra-institutional collective action, and communication. In a palindrome of paradoxes, these stories thus read back around again to plural singularity.

Deep historical narratives of the human condition are also useful for explaining change over time. Here, yet another paradox arises: of necessity and insufficiency – a paradox, I postulate, that is inherent to all dialectical causality in history. None of the basic acts in our existential gamble to enhance our power can be accomplished without simultaneous enactments of all others: Each is necessary to all. Yet no act can be sufficiently explained even by listing all others: Each of these acts always remains "its own thing." Still, our gambles on sustained human existence – that is, human history that stretches across long times and large spaces – are always dialectical. Our power to fend off our vulnerability is produced by mutually constitutive relationships of necessity and insufficiency that make all essential acts of human power and survival possible. I further propose that combinations of such acts – harnessed to each other and to various human purposes including, but not limited to, our gambles on basic survival – should be called "projects."

Projects consisting of actions that are linked necessarily, insufficiently, and in dialectically co-creating interchange are useful for urban historians. As the foundational building blocks of our gambles on basic human survival, these projects elucidate crucial linkages between power, the production of space, and the production of historical time. Deep history contains much concrete evidence of these projects in action. The Pleistocene Epoch, when our species was born – apparently in multiple interacting regions of Africa – offered us approximately 288 tumultuous millennia during which we could deploy our bodily and collective power – driven by our big brains, opposable thumbs, speech and other forms of communication, and our varied, especially large, and often extremely effective social networks – to build shelters capable of mitigating some of our bodies' comparatively weaker features and the many socio-emotional and political difficulties involved in resolving our embodiment with our embeddedness. Our bodily and collective powers rested – necessarily if insufficiently – on the unique power to design shelters and other built structures that allowed us to organize collective movement across vast amounts of space, beyond the comparatively humanophilic conditions of pre-Holocene Africa into colder parts of the world. Shelter also allowed *Homo sapiens* to survive in time, including the Pleistocene's brutally cold "Ice Ages." We even narrowly escaped extinction during decades of extreme planetary cold some 70,000 years ago when ash from Sumatra's Toba volcano shut the sunshine down and reduced the global human population to as few as 10,000 of us. We would not be here without the shelter, the collective sharing of body heat, the coordinated-if-conflictual acts of fuel-harvesting, and the governance of our interactions that got us through that dark "deep" time. Not only that, but over the forty or so millennia that followed, we became one of very few truly global species on Earth, inhabiting all six continents, including regions spanning the equatorial to the Arctic. That feat required immense diversification of our shelters, even if the underlying dialectics of action and power in space and time retained singular attributes that were species-specific (*EP*, Prologue). Deep history thus offers the rawest indication we have of the dialectics involved in the coproduction of human space and power that remained foundational motifs in all subsequent narratives of global urban history. Far from totalistic, these motifs encompass multicausality, multi-directionality, polyrhythms of time, and nested, dialectical paradoxes governed above all by generality and specificity.

Proposition 2: Energy In – Urban Hinterlands

All projects to produce human space and power require harvests and concentrations of energy from the Sun and Earth. Cities require enlarged concentrations of energy, most of it conveyed from non-cities – thinner spaces for harvests, and more threadlike infrastructures for transport to cities. These non-city spaces have always occupied far larger spaces than even the largest cities, and they predate cities in time. They became urban hinterlands whenever, and to the varying degree that, we began To Enlarge and Concentrate – to thicken – the amount of energy in cities. For this reason alone, it follows that all "urbanization" in history has been both "extended" and "differentiated." Theories of "the Urban" useful to historians should be flexible enough to map and taxonomize the many degrees of "urban-ness" which these singularly combined energy-gathering and transporting features of the Urban Condition manifested themselves in space and time.

All cities are planetary. All are situated *on* a planet. All are made *of* a planet. And all exist *at the mercy of* a planet that itself exists in a solar system. All projects of human space production, whether of cities or non-cities, require human projects of energy harvesting from the planet itself and its governing star. The Urban Condition was thus a planetary phenomenon long before it achieved planetary size as Our Urban Planet.

Geologists rightly conceive of Earth's "natural resources" – air, water, food, and fuel; the wood, clay, glass, metal, and stone we use to build our spaces; the human, animal, plant, fungal, and microbiological power that all of these help catalyze – as products of energy that originated in the Sun and transubstantiated into plural forms on, below, or above the surface of Earth over vast courses of geological time. Yet our obligation to harvest energy to produce space is foundationally dialectical, for it obliged us to produce spaces that are situated and designed specifically for varied and changing forms of energy harvest and transport.

During the volatile Pleistocene Epoch, the best design principles for human spaces prioritized spatial mobility: temporary camps, spread out thinly supplemented by more permanent worship and burial sites, fishing and hunting structures, and watering spaces, all connected by semi-permanent trail networks, and later coastal strings of watery inlets lightly modified as harbors. During the Holocene, in a growing number of distinct regions, at dates spread over ten millennia, the new Epoch's less volatile energy flows allowed for a "Neolithic revolution" in human habitat design. Habitats that were fixed in place over longer periods of time, if still thinly dispersed, were necessary for harvests of a growing range of energy forms – notably by means of agriculture and animal domestication. These included villages, farms, and farmhouses, larger indoor and outdoor gathering places, pastures, orchards, fishing and shell-fishing grounds, woodlots, quarries, mines, and waste dumps. Also necessary were more extensive infrastructural spaces designed for transport and communication between dispersed spaces: irrigation ditches, compacted tracks and roads, and expanded strings of river and sea landings. The concentration of water, silt, and nutrient flows in river valleys and estuaries, plus a few other well-watered regions on the fringes of some of them, provided the most prolific sites to produce these village-scapes. River valleys that were particularly narrow because they were hemmed in by energy-poor deserts or mountain chains as in Mesopotamia, Egypt, or Peru, seem to have produced denser agglomerations of villages. In such places, various highly ambiguous and only partially understood contingencies – likely involving Holocenic swings of geo-solar energy in space and time – allowed some of villages to grow, straining our sense of what a village looks like, sometimes becoming what archeologists typically call "towns" (e.g. Jericho, Çatalhöyuk, Banpo) or "mega-sites" (e.g. The Trypillia megasites in Ukraine). Some of these sites may have only been temporarily or seasonally occupied for cultic rites. Sometimes they sustained their larger size for centuries or even millennia, and some arguably enabled their inhabitants to enact some of the specific practices and projects required to produce cities (*EP*, Prologue).

Either way, once cities developed, these typically village-and-town-rich, farm-rich, and transport-infrastructure-rich regions became the first urban hinterlands. The inhabitants of these urban hinterlands delivered increasing portions of the energy that they harvested to fuel the bodies of city dwellers, even as they continued to devote most of those harvests to fuel the bodies of villagers, their animals, and other primary energy harvesters whose thinner spaces remained home to most of the human population until the most recent decades of global urban history. This brings up a key point about the adjective "urban." The "urban" that theorists use most often is typically a "switch-on-switch-off" adjective, with hard boundaries between "inside" and "outside," most often assumed to coincide with the inside and outside of a city itself. Planetary urbanization theorists sought to supersede this common usage by redefining the urban as a function of processes driven above all by capitalist accumulation, not cities. They "extended" the outer boundaries of urban. Sometimes they divided that space into subcategories, but they did not explicitly calibrate ways to measure degrees of urban-ness. To identify the urban nature of non-city, thinner, more threadlike, and even ambiguously thickening city-making spaces, we need an adjective "urban" that, like many other adjectives, recognizes the possibility of variation and degree – and thus the ability to classify spaces as minimally, relatively, and superlatively urban. It is possible, for example, for a thin "rural" or even an "extra-human" space to be "urban" to a minimal degree even if its inhabitants or resident life-forms have never set foot in a city – or even if they have no idea that cities exist – as long as its inhabitants or resident life-forms in some way, even very indirectly, support the production of energy required for a city, even by supplying its own surplus energy to relatively "more urban" non-city-yet-city-making spaces and allowing those spaces in turn to supply cities more directly. In this way, it is possible for historians to draw geographical boundaries, as blurry and ambiguous as they may be, around the outer edges of urban energy-harvesting grids or hinterlands, thus mapping one possible spatial boundary of the Urban Condition at any time. Whenever these combined urban hinterlands reach planetary dimensions, it is also possible to identify one of several possible birthdays of Our Urban Planet.

A concept "urban" that is measurable by degrees also allows us another useful entry point into a crucial paradox of this historical theory. Cities' need for a thickened energy supply – most of which needed to be harvested in thinner spaces and transported through more threadlike ones of varying degrees of urban-ness – is the most obvious way that the Urban Condition came into being, from its historical origins, as both an "extended" and a "differentiated" phenomenon. Again, though its design followed singular basic principles, it was also foundationally plural since at the very least it encompassed contrasting thinner, more threadlike, and thicker spaces.

Meanwhile, spatial distance and historical time added further dimensions of plurality to these otherwise singular design principles for urban hinterlands and the Urban Condition. Simply put, cities were "first" born, largely independently of one another, in many separate birth regions on all continents over many birthdays that span the first five and a half of the six millennia of the history of the Urban Condition. The specific circumstances attending these births varied dramatically, even though, from very early on, city dwellers in a few birth regions interacted in substantial ways with neighboring ones where cities were born earlier – such as in the Indus Valley cities, which from their origins were likely in contact with Mesopotamian ones. In some cases, most notably the Maya lands, specific city-building practices that originated in river-valley hinterlands were transferred to a patchwork of river-poor environments where rainwater had to be gathered in paved reservoirs, cisterns, or seasonal wetlands. Even here, though, no importation of city-producing practice ever took the form of cookie-cutter replication. Indeed, all individual cities in all birth regions also always differed from others in the same region and even the same hinterland (*EP*, chapter 1).

The changing spatial scope and the growing diversity of urban hinterlands mattered immensely to the human condition over time. After 1500, as the World Ocean replaced river valleys as the primary sourcing grounds and delivery devices of city-making geo-solar energy, to be replaced again by deposits of hydrocarbon after about 1780 CE, city-fueling hinterlands became planetary in scope for the first time. Historians should consider these extensions and diversifications of urban hinterlands as foundational material and spatial–political contexts for the radical temporal transformations between the "premodern," "early modern," and "modern conditions" of human experience.

At the same time, spatial differences in the production of new planet-encompassing urban hinterlands also helped produce Our Urban Planet's formative meta-inequalities, those we often abbreviate today as the "uneven development" between (and within) the "Global North" and the "Global South." The growing use of sailing ships to use saltwater currents and winds to deliver oceanic energy to the production of cities was an ancient phenomenon that accelerated everywhere in the world after 1500. However, as I argue in *Earthopolis*, Europe's unique political economic geography and its spatial position in relation to rival urban birthlands as well as the underused Atlantic Ocean gave its mariners, merchants, imperialists, and propagandists incentives and opportunities unlike those of any other river-fed urban birth region to tap energy inputs from the World Ocean as a whole. From there, more importantly, they monopolized the seashores and river valleys of the Americas, as well as the Atlantic trade in enslaved laborers from Africa. While the resulting regional inequalities of energy harvests from the ocean did not immediately transform the geo-political balance between the major legacy river-fed urban regions, they did create the circumstances in which one city, London, was able – and was even compelled – to expand its harvests of hydrocarbon energy from its own even more unique geological hinterland, the coal-rich island of Great Britain (*EP*, chapters 7, 8, and 10).

From there, Europeans, along with the inhabitants of their primary settler colonies and later Japanese city-builders, were able to dominate subsequent harvests of hydrocarbon energy for industry, transport, indoor heating, and agriculture. The vast acceleration in the production of cities and urban hinterlands that followed underlay the enhanced imperial power of the city-propelled states, capitalists, cultural institutions, urban planning institutions, social movements, and other collective forms of action located in what we now know as the Global North. Those inequalities in turn dictated the conditions under which "Global South" cities increased their own imports of hydrocarbon energy, especially after World War II, and the resulting disparities of the "Greatest Acceleration" (or accelerated "extension and differentiation") of cities and urban hinterlands that structure the Urban Planet of Our Time (*EP*, chapters 7, 8, 10, 13, 14, 21–24).

Proposition 3: Cities and Power – To Produce and To Amplify

The production of thick human space matters crucially to human time because it creates conditions especially useful for amplifying human power. To usefully analyze the larger city-producing and city-produced spaces that make up the

Urban Condition over time, we need to retain the classic trio of city-defining *adjectives* larger + denser + more diverse = *thicker* as well as the three adjectives thicker + thinner + more threadlike = the Urban. But sums of adjectives are not sufficient. Henri Lefebvre was right when he included "practices" as central to the "production of space." Verbs are more useful than adjectives to historians as theoretical touchstones, for they are readily observable in our primary sources, and they evoke change, agency, purpose, and causality. Finally, verbs engender more useful temporal narratives – "projects" that link the production of space and human power, notably by amplifying both in cities. Cities, I believe, are best defined by a trio of acts, *To Produce* + *To Amplify* + *To Deploy*. The sum of these three categories of practice allows us to complicate Hannah Arendt's observations about cities and the spatial conditions for power. In Proposition 3, we start with the first two in this triad, *To Produce* and *To Amplify*, dividing each into their component acts and relating them to non-cities, cities, and humans' power to bend both space and time.

The simple proposition that cities should remain at the center of urban history, despite what some leading urban theorists say, leads inexorably into the maw of an old and complicated conundrum: "what, then, is a city?" As part of their critiques of "methodological city-ism," planetary urbanization theorists dismiss many classic answers to this question. Some of these answers are in fact useless, such as any definition of cities that either contains no reference to their relationships with non-city spaces, or more egregiously, argues that cities so thoroughly differ from all other human spaces as to be definable with no context. A second answer revolves around the classic "Chicago School" formula large + dense + diverse, the sum of which, I have proposed, is "thicker." This "theory by adjective" weathered sustained critique long before planetary urbanization theory. Still, I propose retaining it as a skeletal feature of a theory of cities that contextualizes them within the coproduction of thicker, thinner, and more threadlike spaces. A third answer defines cities by means of their so-called "concentration effects." At its most simplistic, this theory posits that larger and denser places are always worth the larger up-front investment because they generate far more output, in the form of "effects" like more wealth, better health and longer lives, greater human creativity and happiness, and more sustainable relationships with nature. Historians and archeologists know that these effects cannot substitute as a full definition of cities, since we have plenty of evidence that concentration can deliver poverty, misery, and death to the majority of city dwellers, and can help urban actors to destroy cities, economies, and ecosystems. Critics of "methodological city-ism" go further and accuse "concentration effects" theorists, correctly in some cases, of exonerating the worst perpetrators of such urban inequalities and violence (Brenner and Schmid, 2015). Still, the possibility that thickened space and concentrated energy create unpredictable historical consequences should make the question of concentration effects far more important and interesting to historians, not less.

This list of inadequate or partially useful answers to "what is a city?" leaves a lot of room for more useful definitions, including ones that handle connections between cities and non-cities better; that more amply address both the causes and consequences of thickness; that better explain the ongoing importance of cities to global urban and human history; and that do so, as I proposed from the outset, by linking the production of space to the production of human power. The key to these more useful definitions is what Lefebvre called "*practices* of urbanization" (Lefebvre, 1970 [2003], 1974 [1991]). Boil that phrase down to its essentials: a theory of "the city" needs *verbs*.

But which verbs? The three I propose – To Produce, To Amplify, and To Deploy – are each "compound" verbs that encompass a range of sub-verbs: they are "boxes" that contain more specific verbs. Theorized as a sum of sums, they add dynamic depth to skeletal definitions of cities that rely on classic three-way sums of adjectives large + dense + diverse = thick (cities), and my own three-way sum thick + threadlike + thin = the Urban Condition. There are useful reasons to explore To Produce, To Amplify, and To Deploy in that order, but note that, like all elements of the theory I propose here, each box of actions, and each act with each separate box, is "its own thing" *and* it is also simultaneously the product as well as a necessary if insufficient producer of all others. As such, it is worth embarking on our "urban theory by verb" by slightly modifying Hannah Arendt's view of cities as the "material origins of power" with this general proposal: Cities are the products and the producers of especially rich *dialectical interactions of actions* essential to the most amplified and diversified deployments of human power in history.

To Produce. The crucial verb in Lefebvre's famous concept "the production of space" does double duty in my proposed theory by verb, for producing space of any kind – whether thicker, thinner, or more threadlike – is crucial to producing human power. We know this already from our excursion into deep history: Producing human space figures among the most basic of the interlocking practices (again, alongside reproduction, care, thought, communication, movement, labor, and so on) that enable us to gamble that our bodily and social powers can minimize the vulnerabilities intrinsic to our uncertain existence on a star-fueled planet. Though To Produce space is connected to these other "deep" actions, it is also its own thing. On top of that, it is also multiple, the sum of its own set of defining sub-verbs. To theorize spatial production and its relation to power production, we could list its component acts in many different sequences, but I propose we start with this further summation: To Produce = To Energize + To Situate + To Design + To Build + To Inhabit.

To Energize. As we already know, the production of all human space, including cities but not limited to them, requires projects of harvesting and moving geo-solar energy. To Energize is itself further made up of a string of verbs that begin with basic deep historical obligations to forage and to harvest; from there to move or to transport; then to accumulate, distribute, and kindle. Finally, humans must *embody* energy in some form or another to allow us to act. To Energize is to plug our human space into the Sun and Earth and, for cities, also to plug our thickest spaces into the available non-city urban hinterlands where, historically, we have harvested the vast bulk of city-producing energy in history. To Energize is also a crucial act in producing all dialectics of space and power – and in igniting any momentum that their mutual coproduction can produce, including any effects on human power produced by spatial concentration.

To Situate (or To Locate). To produce any human space, we also need to determine a placement on the planet that best increases the chances that such a space will best serve the purposes, existential and otherwise, of gambling on the space in the first place. We often explain the site of a village or a city by what may seem like non-human factors, such as the shape of rivers, estuaries, coastlines, or human ones like the presence of built transport routes, but we must also always include willful acts of strategic human decision making. Situating a human settlement is ultimately an act of collective human motiv-ation and purpose: Gambling on a site is a "project." In addition to obvious concerns about access to energy, acts of situating are also important to two other practices specific to the production of cities – To Enlarge and To Concentrate – that I theorize as part of my second box of verbs, To Amplify. Cities grow as enlarged and concentrated clusters around kernels whose original site determines much about the size and shape of the space cities occupy.

To Design. Speaking of shape, the verbs To Design and To Situate are inseparable, since the site of a human space dictates certain design parameters, and because a space's design determines whether the gamble on the site is likely to pan out over time. Some may dispute the idea that all human spaces require acts of design, for we often divide cities into "planned" and "unplanned" ones, hinting that design may not be relevant to the latter. I disagree. Every time we build anything, we always make combined and purposeful decisions about what it will look like and how it can best take advantage of its site. Projects of design can take putatively comprehensive forms, as in an "urban plan," but all production of space requires acts of design, whether all-inclusive or piecemeal.

Crucial general parameters like the thickness, thinness, or threadlike shape of a space are also determined by means of projects of design.

To Build. From there, the foundational necessity of the verb To Build may seem obvious; after all, this is a theory about the production of the "built environment." However, to be theoretically comprehensive as possible, To Build should be conceived broadly to include any kind of human alteration of the preexisting landscape, including digging an irrigation ditch or a mine, plowing a field, or compacting the soil for a track or a street. To Build may thus be better theorized as To Terraform, that is, to rearrange materials from Earth's biosphere and geosphere to meet the human purposes inherent in previous acts of energizing, situating, and design. Building projects, of course, consist of many subsidiary acts, such as those parceled out among history's many building trades. Building is also crucially encompassed within the deeper historical verb to labor, for though many types of labor are not needed for building, building always requires the physical labor of humans, often supplemented by the labor of extra-human animals.

To Inhabit. The last essential act in the production of human space may seem like the most obvious of all. It is, however, also the most complex. Paradoxically, To Inhabit combines acts of movement and lack of movement – "settlement." Habitation of any space requires movement from someplace else. All human structures are also designed for at least some period of acts of narrowed movement on a particular site – what we really mean by settlement – even if that period lasts only for a few days or a season such as in a "non-sedentary" nomadic camp or "semi-sedentary" settlements; or for the combined working, resting, and leisure activities comprised by the entire lifetimes of many generations of people, as in spaces designed for "sedentation" like villages or cities. Vehicles (and animals used as such) are often erroneously ignored in taxonomies of the built environment, but they require various periods of human inhabitation too (especially in long-distance caravans, sea-going ships, or long-haul trucks). Vehicles, of course, also enable movement into, within, and between settlements and their hinterlands that are characteristic of habitation and are critical to their design. In its relation to sedentation, To Inhabit thus implies some relationship with the adjective "permanent," which appears alongside large, dense, and diverse in some iterations of the Chicago School definition of cities (Wirth, 1938), but that also applies to sedentary villages. For a historian, however, the phrase "permanent settlement" begs more questions than it answers, since, as historians well know, no human space is ever "permanent" in the sense that it is immune to radical alteration or complete destruction over time. By contrast, producing all human-built places involves some version of the paradoxical act To Inhabit, a verb that also suitably implies an indeterminate temporality. Another way of noting the complexity of "To Inhabit" when applied to cities, is to theorize that, again unlike "permanent," it contains all the multitudinous interplay of actions and interactions in space, plus our perceptions of both actions and spaces, that Henri Lefebvre theorized – at great length – as the "urban everyday" (Lefebvre, 1968 [1971]).

To Amplify. To produce a *city* from any other form of situated, designed, energized, built, and inhabited human space, we are obligated To Amplify all five of these acts of spatial production, and we must do so in all dimensions. A city, in other words, requires us to amplify the amount and variety of accumulated *energy* forms; the size and thickness of the *design* on or near the original *site*; the amount and variety of *built* things there; the amount and variety of people *inhabiting* the space; and the amount and variety of all action and interaction involved in their habitation of the space. To put this in a "deeper" way, building a city requires projects To Amplify the amount of the very human embodiment and embeddedness that defines both our vulnerability and our power, and we must do so by also amplifying our spatial proximity to one another – whether face-to-face in thickened space, or across more extended and differentiated urban spaces thanks to concentrated energy available for communication and transport. Thus, To Amplify, like To Produce, is a compound verb. Although its components, like those in my other "boxes," can be usefully supplemented or rearranged, I propose this basic equation: To Amplify = To Enlarge + To Concentrate + To Diversify + To Juxtapose + To Catalyze.

To Enlarge + To Concentrate. To theorize the component practices of To Amplify, the first step is a simple-seeming one. We must turn the first two Chicago School adjectives large + dense – the essence of my "thicker" – into verbs that combine as "to thicken," ("to agglomerate" or "to compact" work fine as well). I list To Enlarge and To Concentrate as a conjoined pair because producing a city requires that both happen at once.

As essential to the production of a city as they are, we must note that To Enlarge and To Concentrate are also the source of the primary vexations of urban theory. First, no one has ever been able to say just how big (enlarged) or how dense (concentrated) a human space needs to be to qualify for city-ness. The answer can only be determined in relative temporal and spatial terms. Producing cities requires us To Enlarge a situated inhabited space to a greater degree than other preexisting and surrounding settlements that make cities possible (and that cities make possible) in time and space. Adding to these vexations, by combining To Enlarge with To Concentrate, we also guarantee that cities always occupy far smaller, not larger, spaces than that occupied overall by their thinner hinterlands and forelands (smaller spaces dispersed across a much larger space), and the more threadlike infrastructures (enlarged + elongated + interconnective) that connect cities with the non-cities to create the extended and differentiated space occupied by the Urban Condition.

The best solution to this vexation is to imagine the qualities large and dense as the acts To Enlarge and To Concentrate and accept these acts as central to projects of thickening space that differ with necessarily co-occurring projects of spatial dispersal (the production of even larger thin spaces) and enlargement and elongation (the production of threadlike spaces). Doing so allows us to stretch our mind around another paradox. The sum of the acts To Enlarge and To Concentrate define cities *in relative terms* to non-cities, but these acts also define cities *as universally as possible*. To be sure, no city anywhere or at any time in the historical record ever came into being without projects of design involving simultaneous acts of enlarging and concentrating one situated space relative to the thinner and more threadlike spaces that made the connected urban design project possible in the first place.

A second problem with defining cities by To Enlarge and To Concentrate is that many urban theorists have turned decisively against the Chicago School, claiming that cities themselves have outgrown definitions developed in the mid twentieth century. For some, the theoretical power of large + dense disappeared at some point in the 1990s, in the legendary instant when Henri Lefebvre found himself unmoored in the Los Angeles suburbs, unable to see anything that looked like a city – or more precisely, a "city center" – amidst relentless-seeming low-density sprawl. The "Los Angeles School" that arose from this supposedly revelatory moment kept plenty of enlargement but lost faith in the concentration part. The focus on city "centers" fogged up, and theorists refocused their energy on much "blurrier" peripheries and sharpened their interest in the sheer diversity of urban built forms. This provided fertile ground for the later critique of "methodological city-ism" and the replacement of concentration with concepts of "extended," "differentiated," and even "planetary" urbanism. Breathless lists of non-dense, differentially dense, or indeterminate (again, blurry) urban forms have become common in urban theoretical texts, including this one: "'Suburban,' 'peri-urban,' 'post-suburban,' corridor urbanization, informal settlements, gated communities, tower estates, massive production sites, logistics 'cities,' brutalscapes, deforestation, and vast agricultural landscapes, but also suburban residential sites … kampungs, desakota, peri-urban villages, extensive employment zones, office cities and aeropolises as well as extended recreational and infrastructural spaces" (Tzaninis et al., 2023, 7).

Other lists in this genre keep some focus on city centers, but note that most big cities have become "poly-nodal" urban regions – that is, spaces defined by "multiple centralizations and decentralizations." The newly named

"Urban-Wilderness-Interface" (sometimes called "pyroscapes" given their vulnerability to wildfire) enhances the blurriness of the city, as do spaces interspersed throughout cities and their peripheries where "non-human forces are urbanized" (Tzannis et al., 9). Urban theorists who specifically privilege "situated" points of view "from the Global South" have found much to like in this general anti-Chicago trajectory, noting that focus on central concentration misses the experience of perhaps one third of Earth's urban population. These city dwellers are, after all, responsible for producing one of the most explosive forms of relatively low-density city-making: the self-built or "informal" settlements that surround and pervade most cities in Latin American, Africa, and Asia. Put this way, seeing cities as "thick" can seem like yet another failing of the Eurocentric lens.

Historians are aware of this critique of concentration, but much historical evidence casts doubt on the idea that we live in an especially post-dense urban age. The Greatest Acceleration in the production of cities that ignited in the years around 1945 is indeed a breathtaking phenomenon, especially so in the Global South, where the fastest growing cities are now also distinguished for perhaps the first time in history by the resource-scarcity of their hinterland-city relationships relative to slower-growing ones, not their greater wealth. The scope and causation of this acceleration is indeed unprecedented, and its enormity is worthy of many of the neologisms that theoreticians have invented. Some of these cities have indeed become less dense, even as high-density skyscraper centers also proliferate in more cities than before. Either way, many general design features of spatial production taxonomized in "post-city," "post-metropolitan," or "post-Chicago" theory have existed throughout global urban history. Their scale, and the rates of acceleration at which they achieved that scale varied and never reached that of the last seventy years. However, in their own time, the shape of these forms of "extended urbanism" often elicited similar exclamations of unprecedentedness – and even inspired declarations in their own time that all previous conceptions of the city ought to be scrapped.

That said, any theory of "the city" – such as the one I will offer here – that reclaims the essential role of To Enlarge plus To Concentrate, as a pair, in the spatial production of cities and the Urban Condition must once again reassert the virtues of their *verb* forms. Verbs tell stories that exist in wider contexts of time and space. I repeat that cities always involve some degree of enlargement and concentration over time in relation to what existed previously and elsewhere in thinner or more threadlike spaces that became their hinterlands. Such stories never preclude projects to produce enlarged and concentrated spaces that vary dramatically in size or that vary in thickness – either internally or relative to other enlarged and concentrated spaces that exist at the same time.

Henri Lefebvre, I submit, could well have had a very similar ah-ha moment about the variability of urban concentration in otherwise enlarged cities of the very distant past. Plunk him down in the extramural informal settlements or urban orchards of Babylon, and he could have had equal trouble locating a center, even though the very "Tower of Babel" lurked not too far away. The same could have been true if he visited Plato's Academy in ramshackle suburban Athens; or the vast *suburbium* of ancient Rome; or on one of the outlying islands of West Africa's archipelagic city of Djenné Djenno; or in the farmer's fields contained within the walls of either Han or Tang Changan for much of their existence; or at an aristocratic estate on the massive semi-dense peripheries of Mayan Tikal or Angkor; let alone along the docklands of eighteenth-century Amsterdam or London; in the sinuous alleys of Calcutta's "Black Town" that so mystified Europeans, or the sprawling centerless working-class districts of Manchester whose unprecedented extent and isolation Friedrich Engels described with such great exclamation; or, indeed the then-unprecedented suburban sprawl around Louis Wirth's early twentieth-century Chicago itself. Like all cities in history, all these places were, in fact, variably thick: Most had multiple centers or "nuclei" (at the very dawn of global urban history, the city of Uruk came into being around at least two centers). All cities have likewise been segregated to various degrees and in multiple ways that reflect often obscene inequalities of investment and differential density within cities and their peripheries. Even cities with supposedly distinct boundaries marked by walls often had extensive indeterminate lower-density peripheries – whether within those walls or outside them. Like today, these included spaces that were above all residential, mercantile, industrial, military, agricultural, or infrastructural, or, for that matter, heavily invaded by extra-human species. The blurriness – even sloppiness – of urban nuclei, intervening spaces, outer boundaries, and peripheries is a fact of all cities, not only of cities in our own time. At the same time, it is also a dimension on which cities differ from each other, nearly infinitely over time and in space.

That said, no theorist looking around from any of the places I have just listed could remotely deny that they were positioned within the thickest built space anywhere else in the region and/or its recent past – if not in the world as a whole and in all previous history to that point. Today, the same is true. Even the most extended – or even "distended" – cities in the Global North or Global South, sprawling as they may be, remain denser than most of the far thinner spaces that make up vast, overlapping, now planet-sized urban hinterlands that still harvest most of the basic energy for all denser places, even as many of these city-creating non-cities have grown far denser during the Greatest Acceleration too, relative to earlier times. The same is true of the more threadlike infrastructures that convey most of that human-harvested energy toward all the world's densest places: These non-cities may have thickened too, and even grown thicker city-like nodes of their own, but their basic purposes require them to retain an overall far more elongated, far less thickened – again, less concentrated – form than the cities they supply.

This is the advantage of starting with a conception of the Urban based on the histories of practices that produce urban hinterlands and that proceed to practices of city-production through acts of amplification that those hinterlands make possible. To repeat a point that I made at the outset: The Urban has always been and always will be extended and differentiated as well as blurry; the places within an extended and diverse city-producing space where the most enlargement and concentration occur are those with the likeliest credentials for the title cities, no matter how internally differentiated or extended or blurry those thicker spaces are.

There is more. Applied to cities, the verbs To Enlarge and To Concentrate must refer to more than the design of the hard built environment itself – the evidence that ultimately undergirds most "city" – minimizing theories of extended and differentiated urbanization. To Enlarge and To Concentrate are acts that amplify the thickness of all acts required for city production – including not only the acts of situating, designing, and building that bring hard structures into being but also acts of energizing and inhabiting. Thickness of energy and people in space are just as crucial as thickness of built structures in the historical relationship between thickened space and amplified power. Sum together more energy + more human bodies + more human embeddedness alone, and the resulting amplification of human power produced by thickened action and interaction requires theory too – even a prominent seat in urban theory more generally. As we shall see in Proposition 5 on urban forelands and Our Urban Planet, amplified power in thick spaces – cities – is not only the product but also a critical determinant of the quantity and design of thinner and more threadlike space.

The next three verbs in my box marked To Amplify typically – if not always – follow To Enlarge + To Concentrate, even if they often also make more enlargement and concentration of space possible. They supplement and extend the dialectical yet contingent relationship between the amplification of thick space, energy, building, and habitation, and the amplification of human power.

To Diversify. The relationship of non-city hinterlands to cities is crucial for this city-defining act – a verb obviously derived from the Chicago School's third adjective "diverse." The verb form To Diversify is meant to convey human acts of amplifying diversity over time, typically in dialectical relationship to projects of enlargement and concentration. Once hinterlands produce more energy than is necessary for the sustenance of other primary producers alone, that "surplus" can "accumulate" – that is, *enlarged* amounts of energy can *concentrate* – in thick places best situated and designed for habitation by people who are free to do something other than produce primary energy. People there can thus engage in projects to specialize their activities, notably their occupations, amplifying their scope and diversity with concentrated and diversified energy forms available to accomplish them, as well as the built structures and spatial designs required. If those projects of diversification result – as they often did through further acts that we will explore soon – in technologies that increase the efficiency of hinterland-based energy-production further, more people from more diverse parts of non-city hinterlands can move and settle in cities, thickening them further. Cultural, linguistic, cultic, religious, "ethnic," "racial," and class diversity can increase alongside diversity of specialized occupational activity in large, concentrated places. Not only is diversified specialization a likely outcome of plugging thicker spaces into thinner ones, documentation of this sequence of acts exists profusely in the global urban historical record. Conversely, acts of urban destruction or collapse in regional accretions of the Urban Condition also predictably resulted in acts of comparative homogenization and de-specialization of activity, as reversion to thinner places results in de-specialization and a return to the primacy of primary energy production. While it is true that imperial and capitalist projects initiated in the Global North have also turned cities into forces of global cultural homogenization, the world's thickest spaces – in both the North and the South – have also simultaneously spawned new hybrid identities, cultures, and practices, which have further diversified as they spread and mix worldwide, also mostly thanks to cities.

To Juxtapose. That said, projects of spatial production that combine enlargement, concentration, and diversification alone do not always guarantee the next crucial verb in the dialectics of amplification: To Juxtapose. Jane Jacobs, the greatest theorist (and enthusiast) of urban juxtaposition, noted that the specific design of urban space matters to the likelihood of potentially power-amplifying human-scale, face-to-face interactions between diverse people – juxtapositions – that cities promise. Jacobs's famous critiques of "international modernist" urban design, as embodied by her nemesis, the New York City planner Robert Moses, focused on his plans to destroy neighborhoods where many juxtaposed activities occurred in human-scale spaces within walkable or bikeable distances. He determined to segregate "urban functions" – residence, work, leisure, commerce, industry, and transport – to different spaces in the city that were inaccessible to each other, minimizing the juxtaposition of city-diversified activities (Jacobs, 1961).

Yet precisely because To Juxtapose is a practice that city builders can shut off, the verb also allows us to reassess another definition of cityhood – that proposed by theorists of "concentration effects." The microeconomists and economic geographers who developed this concept most recently were inspired by Jacobs's observations on juxtaposition (some nickname these effects "Jane Jacobs effects"). As in many theories proposed by social scientists, concentration effects theory began as a statistical variable, in this case designed to account for the fact that, given similar microeconomic inputs, urban economies extravagantly outperformed those of less concentrated settlements, even though cities have thus far in history been unable to produce enough energy on site for their own populations (Harris, 2021, 16–26). Molecular explanations for these statistical impacts of concentrated space on output-amplification include the following. (1) The lowering of transport costs in environments thick with people allows a greater volume and frequency of human interaction. (2) The diversified forms of specialized work in thick spaces allows for greater volumes of beneficial commercial interchanges between specialists as well as the cross-fertilization of innovative imagination, ideas, and practices, leading to innovation and more specialization – what Jacobs called "new forms of work" (Jacobs, 1969). (3) Concentrated places allow for economies of scale and larger production spaces that allow for efficiencies boosted by the division of labor. (4) Cities facilitate the development of larger niche markets for cutting edge goods and services that can help finance innovation over extended and often unpredictable periods of technological development. (5) Cities can support "thinking places" – coffee shops, bookstores, publishing houses, libraries, museums, theaters, schools, university campuses, and the like – involving actors with more points of view capable of higher quality brainstorming or the more efficient use of the human "social brain." (6) These spaces also increase locals' capacity to import, mix, store, and disseminate knowledge to and from elsewhere. (7) Cities thus attract "creatives" with far greater impact on the economy than places that do not attract them or even repel them. (8) Space – in the form of urban land or built structures – increases in value to suit its many possible profitable uses, creating new pools of capital for larger-scale investments. (9) Cities allow far greater efficiencies of energy use including the heating of dense structures and in transport. (10) For all these reasons, wages for labor rise compared to those in non-cities, stimulating far greater consumption, output, and accumulation of wealth.

The problem with these microeconomic data is not with the data itself – some urban historians and even archeologists have found it possible to replicate similar effects using far sparser datasets from the past (e.g. Smith, 2019). The problem is the use of this data to make far grander historical conclusions, including, most extravagantly, Edward Glaeser's pronouncement that cities always make us "richer, smarter, greener, healthier, and happier" than non-cities (Glaser, 2010). Stopping somewhat short of that, the theorist Edward Soja extoled what he called the "synekesis" (from *synecoia*, a concept linked to the Greek *polis*), and the architectural historian Spiro Kostof used the vivid image of "energized crowds" (Kostof, 1991) to describe the exponential amplification of activities and outputs possible in cities. Both conceived of the effects of what Soja called "the stimulus of urban agglomeration" in more open-ended ways than Glaeser, however; Soja rightly cautioned, somewhat reluctantly in his case, that "synergisms could be both "creative" and "occasionally destructive" (Soja, 2000, 12).

Urban historians have frequently commented on the causal relationship between juxtaposition and amplification. Yet we too must exercise caution and note the many possible paths that can follow from To Enlarge, To Concentrate, To Diversify, and To Juxtapose. To start, our archives amply and repeatedly confirm Jacob's own observation that urban designers can switch juxtaposition on or off, even in the thickest and most diverse of cities. On top of that, proximity of position in space alone does not guarantee anything predictable at all, even in the thickest space. As Richard Sennett observed correctly, most face-to-face encounters in cities – by far – occur between people who do not know each other and who arguably communicate little of any consequence with each other. Cities could just as easily be defined by Sennett's phrase, "the milieu of strangers," as places of "energized crowds" – and, worse, as zones of energy-sapping loneliness, anonymity, or the "boredom" that Lefebvre noted in the "everyday" (Lefebvre, 1968 [1971]), or even Durkheim's "anomie." Finally, as we have seen, cities can also produce forces of homogenization as well as diversification.

To Catalyze. Something else needs to happen for juxtaposition to produce *energized* crowds in thickened spaces, rather than groups of depressed people or concentrations of non-interacting strangers. I chose the verb To Catalyze carefully because I believe that it is useful for historians to take notice when our evidence indicates that urban actors have, in fact, seized upon the advantages created by an enlarged, concentrated, diversified, and juxtaposed space to do something as an "embedded" human force that they could not do in more thin or threadlike spaces. As in chemistry labs where the term originated, To Catalyze also rightfully implies that both a "crucible"-like space – the city itself – and specific purposeful interactions or reactions are required for that space to produce amplified human power. To Catalyze, furthermore, better expresses the possibility that amplifications of power can result from conflict – or thicker concentrations of energy alone – than To Synergize, which implies that power grows only from human alignment or "virtuous cycles."

What we should expect from any historically verifiable marriage of thick space and catalyzed power, though, is not any predictable "concentration effect," but a search for further evidence of what happened next. Here, the historical record does not lie. At times, projects of catalysis in cities did result in greater wealth, new knowledge, better ways of relating to nature, longer more fulfilling human lives, more human life on Earth, and perhaps larger energized and inspired crowds to come: moments when To Catalyze resulted in To Synergize, as Soja predicted. However, we cannot get so bewitched by our subject that we ignore evidence that the effects of "concentration" can also include poverty, inequality, oppression, ignorance, falsehood, environmental disaster, misery, and death – not to mention the destruction of whole cities themselves. Even at moments in the historical record when urban juxtaposition does make some of us "richer, smarter, greener, healthier, and happier," the same cities and crowds are historically far more likely to produce those outcomes most copiously for a few – and deny them cruelly to most.

The reason for this unpredictability is simple: The only truly predictable "effect" of "concentration" is also its principal cause – the production and amplification of *power*. As raw "force-multipliers," cities do not release us from the conditions of the existential gamble that led us to produce them. Catalyzing more human power may allow us to raise the stakes in our dependence on other humans, other life-forms, and the Sun and Earth, but more power does not guarantee any enhanced payoff, favorable or otherwise. What our archives tell us is only this: "energize" a "crowd" or "multiply" a "force" in space, and anything can follow. As Colson Whitehead (2021) put it wisely: "The city clutched everything in its grasp and spread it every which way. Maybe you had a say in which direction, and maybe you didn't."

So true. But our urban theory "by verb" still has a bit of predictive power left in its tank, if only to explain Whitehead's urban unpredictability. Once we produce and amplify power in cities, cities also predictably force us – and predictably diversify the means that make it possible for us – To Deploy it.

Proposition 4: Predictably Unpredictable – To Deploy

The production and amplification of human spatial power has only one sure "effect": We deploy that space and that power, and in predictably unpredictable ways. Our third "box" of city-defining verbs contains not a clear list of discrete action words, but several wide ranges of practice. Deploying spatial power requires combining many, often contradictory acts into strategic projects whose unforeseeable collisions and outcomes set the unpredictable conditions – within history – of cities' complex dialectical relationships to such power-deploying entities as states, social movements, accumulations of wealth, knowledge production and dissemination, collective mobility, and reproduction – and from there to the production of larger urban forelands. Open the box marked To Deploy, and we must ask: At what point does urban theory yield to untheorizable furies only knowable as global urban history?

To Deploy. Acts of deploying urban spatial power lie in an epistemological space where urban theory's predictive powers trail off. These acts are accordingly more difficult to classify than acts of production and amplification. First, To Deploy is best conceived not by a discrete set of component verbs, but as overlapping ranges of action that stretch between pairs of conflicting opposites. I sum these verb-spectrums thus: *To Align* through *To Differentiate* + *To Negotiate* through *To Conflict* + *To Distribute* through *To Appropriate* + *To Narrate* through *To Counter-Narrate* + and *To Govern* through *To Disrupt*. Second, deployment of spatial–political power requires *projects* – again, combinations of acts at once purposeful and strategic, improvisational, inherently contingent, and dialectical, all coproductive of each other in necessary but insufficient ways. The exact combinations of these acts matter to projects of power deployment, but those combinations also factor into the increasing untheorizability of the verb To Deploy. Third, to include To Deploy in a theory of the city, we must further qualify Hannah Arendt's theory about cities as the material basis for power. Residents of non-cities were perfectly able to deploy power by means of projects that include all these ranges of verbs. To Deploy only becomes an essential component of a theory *of the city* when acts of deployment occur in dialectical relationships with projects of spatial–political amplification. Fourth, that said, the availability of amplified power in cities at once obligates and enables deployers of urban power to further diversify the combinations, strategies, dialectics, and contingencies otherwise involved in all projects of space–power deployment – resulting, for example, in a greater variety of projects of state-formation, wealth accumulation, and collective cultural practice. Multiplied and diversified deployment projects like these, involving more diverse "energized crowds," result in multiplied and diversified possible outcomes. Cities' greatest effects are thus ever more predictably unpredictable – theorizable only as dwindling theorizability.

To their credit, urban theorists have long sought to theorize cities' genius for slipping away from theory's grasp. In the 1940s, some resorted to insights from "complexity theory," originally meant to explain molecular interactions in volatile substances. The foundational metaphor of complexity theory was a billiard table on which multiplying numbers of balls travel in essentially random directions, creating unpredictable patterns of collision and subsequent directionality (e.g. Weaver, 1947). The observation that the serial effects of these balls' encounters with each other were as real yet as increasingly complex as they became less predictable helps us to imagine how simultaneous projects of power deployment align and collide in thickened space. Neo-Marxist theorists have been somewhat less comfortable with urban unpredictability. They see "crisis" as a structural result of the deployment of power via processes of capital accumulation in cities, but they count on cities to "fix" things spatially, resolving the lapse in predictability caused by crisis. More recently, scholars who examine cities from a postcolonial or Global-South perspective have emphasized the inability of Eurocentric theory to grasp the normality and contradictory nature of what AbdouMaliq Simone calls the "provisional" and "turbulent" nature of "the urban condition" (Simone, 2022). Mirroring the opposing pairs of verbs that I have proposed as defining components of To Deploy, Simone uses the contradictory concept "(dis)order" to define this turbulence – and urges us not to seek refuge in "solutions" for it, but to grow epistemologically comfortable with "things affecting and being affected by others in ways that are always uncertain, open, and multiple" (Simone, 2022). Edward Soja, one source of Simone's inspiration, offered a more precise map of the road beyond the edge of theory. His idea of "Thirdspace" – an abstraction of an already abstract, three-part concept of the city proposed by Henri Lefebvre – names an epistemological zone where "practice" (Lefebvre's first component of cityhood and Soja's "Firstspace") and Lefebvre's second component ("thoughts about space," or Soja's "Secondspace") refract each other in kaleidoscopic and "perhaps unknowable" ways. Where do our epistemological paths lead at the point when cities become "unknowable" by theoretical means? "The best we can do," Soja counsels, "is selectively explore ... the infinite complexity of life through its intrinsic spatial, social, and *historical* dimensions" (Soja, 2000, 12).

The emphasis on "historical" is my own. Soja's statement is poignant for those of us who devote our lives to the scholarly field of urban history. Over the past fifty years or so, we have collectively produced thousands of volumes of no-doubt "selective" – yet also reasonably "knowable" – knowledge about cities in "historical dimensions." Our knowledge-production process hinges for the most part on the basic professional practice of visiting archives and opening boxes of vestiges of the past. What comes out of these boxes, I am quite convinced, can in fact be usefully theorized by something that looks quite like my box of verbs marked To Deploy. The contradictory archival furies that fly at this outer limit of theories of complexity, "(dis)order," or "Thirdspace," are quite familiar to urban historians as basic evidence. Unlike billions of bouncing billiard balls, these furies are made up of ranges of purposeful acts which historical actors in cities attempt, as best as their measure of urban-amplified power allows, to assemble into "ordered" strategic projects of power deployment. All along, these actors know very well that the internal contradictions intrinsic to acts of power deployment, and the collisions any such project will predictably experience with other projects of greater or lesser power, will force those actors to improvise or create new, often "provisional" or "(dis)ordered" versions of their projects, even as they redefine or re-narrate the guiding purposes of their projects while they press forward.

Can we theorize these furies beyond their predictable unpredictability, and in ways that are useful to global urban historians? My proposal is that we dig deeper into ranges of verbs that make up projects of power deployment, while also encouraging readers to vary and grow the list.

Between To Align and To Differentiate. This spectrum of verbs refers to the discursive and social business of mustering people – of "embedding" "embodied" human beings, to use my "deeper" terminology – required by all projects of human space–power deployment. To Align is a highly aspirational place to start this list. There is no question that acts of forming deployable group identities by defining a hopefully sizable and thus powerful "We" matters to the basic formation of projects of power deployment, especially so in thick, diversified spaces. As part of his definition of cities and "social complexity," the archeologist Vere Gordon Childe even speculated that cities were places where such acts of alignment took new forms, centered on an occupational specialty, say, or a space rather than kinship, say, or the opposition of settlers vs. nomads (Childe, 1950). The growing consensus in paleoanthropology is that the range of acts of alignments in cities likely overlapped far more with those in non-city or even pre-city societies (e.g. Graeber and Wengrow, 2021), an interpretation that rhymes well with a theory of the Urban that focuses on the mutual creation of thin, threadlike, and thicker spaces. Either way, the opposite of To Align – that is, To Differentiate – is just as important. It differs from To Diversify, the component of amplification, in that To Differentiate involves the deployment of real power on the part of a "We" to identify an opposed "Them," paradoxically creating a project of alignment defined by its opposition to a power-deploying Other. In history, projects of power deployment typically combine various shifting emphases on alignment and differentiation. In cities, they may keep characteristics of similar projects empowered in non-cities, but they also multiply in tune with acts of settlement enlargement and concentration; they diversify as all things tend to do in thicker places; they juxtapose in their larger and more diverse forms against each other in space if that space is designed to facilitate juxtaposition; and they interact and sometimes catalyze with many more other projects of alignment and differentiation than they would in a village or along a threadlike roadside. As acts of deployment, the strategies and purposes involved in alignment and differentiation also multiply, requiring another range of verbs.

Between To Negotiate and To Conflict. All projects involving power deployment require acts of purposeful strategy-making. Unlike careening billiard balls that have no will of their own, projects of alignment and differentiation must also consciously align their strategies with a purpose: an outcome that is worth the gamble. Acts of negotiation and conflict encompass a wide range of possibilities, from settling differences with competing projects, to forging alliances of convenience, to the construction of coalitions between projects along principles of "no-permanent-friends/no-permanent-enemies," to direct collisions involving a further wide range of possible practices – from attack narratives to institutional maneuver to physical violence. Combinations of negotiation and conflict typically add much to the unpredictability of any interaction of differently aligned power projects, and all multiply in cities. Accordingly, these acts can catalyze further unforeseeable possibilities of action – that is, power.

Between To Distribute and To Appropriate. Projects to deploy human power can have many missions or purposes, but they almost always include the acquisition and/or the disposition of further measures of power (or energy, wealth, ideas, or human numbers) itself. Projects whose purpose is To Distribute power more equitably can do so as an end in themselves, or to widen the "embedded" power of their aligned members. Far too many projects of deployment in urban history instead sought To Appropriate power in the hands of smaller groups of people who further align around preserving their superior grabs of power. Most often, power deployment involves combinations of distribution and appropriation. We now know well that humans in pre-city societies were also capable both of acts of highly egalitarian distribution and highly inegalitarian acts of appropriation. In cities, amplified stocks of available energy and power raise the stakes of these distributions and appropriations and, I theorize, they predictably add diversity, intensity, and unpredictability to the outcomes of these projects and their impacts on the space occupied by the Urban Condition and the experience of inhabiting it. City space itself – a product as well as a producer of amplified power – is heavily affected by acts of distribution and appropriation. So-called urban "morphological" features, like nucleation, segregation, and boundedness – not to mention urban extendedness, differentiation, and blurriness – are not static things or "definitive" features of cities as some theorists argue: They reflect strategic acts of design that are components of projects of distribution and appropriation of space and power. They are historical phenomena, best understood not by means of snapshot statistical "indexes" of nucleation or segregation for example, but as always evolving, unmeasurable and unpredictable furies of power deployment in space and time (e.g. Nightingale, 2012).

Between To Narrate and To Counter-Narrate. In history, the realm Soja called "Secondspace" – based on Lefebvre's "thoughts about space" – actually lies thoroughly within "Firstspace," the realm of spatial practice. The verbs To Narrate and To Counter-Narrate are "practices" themselves, not only critical to the generation of "urban imaginaries," but also essential to all other projects of deploying space and power. To Narrate also has "deeper" roots in humans' ability to derive embodied and embedded power from our species' prodigious talents for communication. Acts like To Align and To Differentiate cannot happen in the absence of narratives and counter-narratives about "we" and "they." Narratives are essential for articulating shared strategic choices involved in negotiation and conflict. And given the unpredictable outcomes of power deployment, narratives are essential to legitimating the purposes of our projects, whether centered on distribution or appropriation. To Narrate and To Counter-Narrate play roles in human power deployment projects that occur in non-cities as well as cities. In history, however, cities have allowed opportunities for the mixing and storage of more diverse forms of knowledge as well as dissemination over larger spaces, most often giving an upper hand to narratives and counter-narratives developed in cities over those in non-cities (virtual spaces may weaken cities' historic upper hand in matters of narration). Cities are also a historical precondition for the development of narratives that compare the moral and political traits of cities and non-cities. These "morality tales" about city and country are thus a foundational feature of the Urban Condition, with great importance for projects of power deployment (more in Proposition 7).

Between To Govern and To Disrupt. The best-known way for humans to deploy power is by producing institutions and social movements, though other forms of collective actions are also critical, often superseding the power of institutions and movements. Projects of institution or movement building hinge on normative narratives that guide practices of power deployment, including alignment and differentiation, negotiation and conflict, distribution, and appropriation, and how to handle counter-normative narratives. The verb *To Govern* refers to relatively successful projects to deploy power through institutions that claim legitimacy through such narratives of "order" – typically involving law, official propaganda, administrative routines, and institutional monopolies on violence – and minimize unpredictable or counter-normative deployment projects. Such institutionalized governance "solutions," to use Simone's words, never fully eradicate political "turbulence" – least of all perhaps in cities – but in history their justificatory narratives have often allowed institutional actors to impose alignment with the institution on a large scale – if only as "organized chaos," another useful term from complexity theory. The verb *To Disrupt* refers to projects to delegitimize these kinds of institutional order, using counter-narratives to build large-scale alignments, movements, or collective acts that reverse appropriations of power necessary for institutional governance.

A theory that defines cities as humans' most consequential spaces for the production, amplification, and deployment of power predicts that cities are also essential to the production of humans' most powerful institutions and social movements. One of the advantages of a *historical* theory of cities is that it can examine whether the historical evidence supports this theory. From what I learned while writing *Earthopolis*, the answer is an overwhelming, if qualified, "Yes." Most of the most powerful institutions and social movements in world history thus far – measured by the number of people they have affected, the scope of the space they have affected, and their consequences on change over time – have relied foundationally upon cities for the power they deploy.

These institutions include those we typically associate with "governance," like states of all kinds (city-states, empires, and national states, whether authoritarian or formally subject to the consent of the governed), but also those that specialize in governance of wealth accumulation (merchant houses, firms, cooperatives, communes, and capitalist corporations), and those that specialize in governance of culture or knowledge (temple cults, organized religions, consumer cultures, academic and educational institutions, and propaganda mills). City-empowered social movements too are various and – from new interpretations of archeological evidence – may be as old as city-empowered governing institutions: They include a wide variety of anti-authoritarian, redistributionist, counter-cultural, counter-hegemonic, and environmental movements that advocate everything from piecemeal reform of governing institutions to their revolutionary overthrow. The social movements with the greatest impact on our own time are those that abolished Atlantic slavery; that overthrew authoritarian, absolutist, or totalitarian governing institutions, replacing them with institutions formally based on the consent of ever-greater proportions of the governed; and that sought to reverse the power of capitalists by various radical experiments in state ownership of the means of production. These movements are associated with the modern era, but historians of premodern periods and archeologists have discovered increasing evidence of urban social movements that may have helped found the earliest cities, even reversing authoritarian regimes thought to be pervasive in the period (e.g. Graeber and Wengrow, 2021).

These same bodies of evidence require us to leave considerable airspace between the history of cities and the histories of governing institutions and disruptive social movements. The history of states is a good example. Long entombed in the same theoretical sarcophagus marked "civilization" alongside cities, "complex societies," money, writing, and so on, states are in fact, of course, their own thing – easily as complicated as cities and subject to equally vexed theorization. My preference is to theorize the relationship between the "production of space" and "state formation" – and for that matter between cities and "capital accumulation" or cities and "civilization" – as still another example of dialectics built around principles of necessary-yet-insufficient coproduction. Both cities and states can be usefully, if only partly, defined by the ranges of verbs in my box marked To Deploy. However, the best evidence we have is that non-city spaces were perfectly suited for the development of many elements of institutions we might think of as states, including combinations of alignment and appropriation we like to call "kingship," "charismatic rule," or "cultic regimes" that deployed power over multiple households and kinships typically known To Govern the earliest, most dispersed and most mobile non-city habitats. All such institutions persisted in cities, even as other elements of states came into being there more often – including bureaucracies, tax-collection practices, courts, economic regulation systems, and standing armed forces – along with the typically larger built structures required to sustain them. Indeed, it is possible that our abstract concept of "state" itself rests so heavily on the historical urban accumulation of these elements of governing institutions that they obscured non-city antecedents that had fewer or smaller versions of these elements but equally plausible claim to the concept "state" (Graeber and Wengrow, 2021). Moreover, it is not a foregone conclusion that cities ever required "states" at all, either for their production or To Govern their amplified size, energy harvests, or power deployments. In *Earthopolis*, I highlight the classic case of a "stateless" (or "self-organized") city, ancient Djenné-Jenno in the Niger Bend of Africa, a space described with much insight by the archeologist Roderick McIntosh (McIntosh, 2006). Because such cities leave fewer archeological traces, they may have been more numerous than we know. Lastly, states typically appropriated the power concentrated in cities for their own projects, while muzzling cities by granting them subsidiary or "municipal" institutions that typically possessed little power over non-city spaces in urban hinterlands (or forelands). In that way, states acquired a somewhat arbitrary but widely shared power to determine which thicker settlements of various sizes and densities qualified as "cities," creating yet another massive vexation for urban theorists.

The example of states illustrates a final qualification to any effort to link cities with history's most powerful institutions and social movements. While it is true that cities amplified state power more than other types of settlements, the power wielded by city-based states was never absolute or without rivals. In history, nomadic camps and villages could also, quite often, enable their inhabitants to deploy amplified power that could rival and oppose that of very powerful city-based states, in many cases destroying both. Peasant revolts and village-based sea-raiders like the Vikings destroyed many cities and weakened or overthrew the states based there. Arguably, the single most powerful state in premodern times came not from mighty cities of the rivers, but from the yurts of the Central Asian grasslands, an ideal space for amplifying the power of horse-mounted warriors. Mongol cavalries laid waste to cities across large swaths of Afro-Eurasia, and they administered their "Hordes" from tented camps, complete with mobile yurt-palaces, migrating north and south along the rivers of north central Asia and taxing merchants bearing goods from West to East at various strategic river crossings. Though the khans did build city-like "places" such as Qaraqorum and Sarai, they primarily did so to meet visiting ambassadors from sedentary city-based regimes to renegotiate terms of trade and taxation (Favereau, 2021).

The Mongol Empire is the greatest exception to the rule that cities are required for history's most powerful deployments of administrative and armed power. However, it proves the rule too – for in many ways the Mongol Empire was as much a creation of the Urban Condition as a destroyer of it. It is unlikely that the camp-dwelling clans who established these empires would have been able to coalesce in the first place without the promise of looting urban riches. The Mongols' weapons, notably their gunpowder ones, were only available because of technological advances in cities. The khans' taxation of the east-west trade relied on city-amplified wealth and city-anchored long-distance commerce in city-made luxuries. Indeed, by promoting trans-Eurasian trade, the Mongols helped develop the power of city-based states, notably Russia, not to mention the vast city-based state the Mongols governed themselves, the Yüan Dynasty of China (Favereau, 2021).

The role Hannah Arendt assigns to cities as humans' foremost spatial producers of power was thus pervasive but nonetheless historically contingent, especially in premodern times. It was only in the early-modern era that a city-based state, the Qing dynasty – itself a governing force that first arose in sparser places – finally ended Asian cities' millennia-old rivalry with nomadic states. Still, ever since then, numerous insurgencies based in much thinner spaces, helped by the proliferation of city-produced weapons, have repeatedly harassed and overthrown city-based governments, including most recently in the city of Kabul. In this context, it is also worth noting that in our own time, cities have a new rival as our principal power-producing spaces: so-called "virtual space." Like nomadic empires and sea raiders, virtual spaces depend on cities and threadlike infrastructures only possible because of cities. As such, they too must be considered, at least in part, urban. Yet, like other rival means of amplifying human power, virtual spaces also derive their power from beyond cities – from internet-based social platforms, their data-gathering capacities, the algorithms that process this data, and the artificial "intelligence" they make possible. All these features of virtual space can out-catalyze knowledge-creation projects in urban physical spaces, and thus potentially deploy highly disruptive city-based political, economic, and cultural power. Virtual spaces' capacity to disseminate disinformation may even be less predictable than projects of narration and counter-narration deployable from cities, bringing into question the hard-won historical dominance of urban-based institutions, including democratic social movements, over human affairs.

Notice what has happened here: the ability of a theory by verb to predict the spatial power of cities, let alone any theory of the state, capitalism, culture, "civilization," social movements, revolution, human mobility, or human repro-duction has trailed off. By displaying the contradictory contents of the box of verbs marked To Deploy, however, we do get a theoretical bonus. The contents of that box explain how cities themselves set the outer limits of their own theorizability – and from there lead us into a wide realm of historical contingency.

These fraying ends of a theory of the *city*, however, do not mark the outer boundaries of a theory of the *urban*. Just as the production of cities requires larger urban spaces to harvest inward flows of energy, so city-amplified deploy-ments of power reach outward, often far beyond city limits, affecting other cities and non-cities anew. In this way, such projects can expand or contract the space occupied by the Urban Condition; recently, these projects have added momen-tum to its accelerations to planetary scope. To usefully interpret the history of spaces of urban-power outflow, we need still more urban theory. Specifically, we need to dramatically widen the scope of global urban history to include urban forelands.

Proposition 5: Power Out – Urban Forelands

What we know so far: Cities are places where we harvest geo-solar energy to produce, amplify, and deploy space and our power as a species on Earth. What comes next? (1) Our actions – deployed through institutions, movements, or other large-scale collective projects – take up space in themselves, within cities and beyond them, creating *Realms of Action*. (2) Our actions require that we produce new human spaces – thin, threadlike, and thick alike – and sometimes destroy them, building *Realms of Habitat*. (3) Our Realms of Action and Habitat, in turn, also transform extra-human spaces within and beyond human space: *Realms of Impact*. (4) Those impacts, finally, are reflected in the amount of human and extra-human life and death on Earth, a benefit or a cost which also takes up space: *Realms of Consequence*. Our theories of cities may have run their course, but we can still theorize the spaces that *cities make possible*: urban forelands, and the Realms of Action, Habitat, Impact, and Consequence.

Return once again to Colson Whitehead's hard-bitten words: The city "took everything into its clutches," and then it "sent it every which way." Urban theorists and historians may grudgingly agree that "clutching everything" qualifies as an *urban* phenomenon – it is the business of urban hinterlands. We are less primed to accept the urban-ness of the space that Whitehead calls "sending every which way." But the proposition that cities must be defined by verbs To Amplify and To Deploy demands that we deem spaces created by outward flows of human power as *urban* spaces too. Concepts like "extended urbanization" and "differentiated urbanization" suggest one possible geographic classification. But in planetary urbanization theory, these concepts primarily map *built* space and, of that, space produced to meet the needs of capital accumulation. Admittedly that amounts to a lot of urban space, but it is not remotely equivalent to "everything" in global urban historical time, let alone "every which way" in planetary space.

Using the term "urban forelands" for outward-extending spaces that cities make possible may, at first, seem unpromising. After all, these spaces are not solely the creation of cities. People, in their role as state actors, wealth accumulators, knowledge producers, and social movement activists, play principal roles in making these spaces possible too, and so have more generalized groups of people or groups of households who move *en masse* from one part of the world to another, or who behave in collective ways that either augment or diminish our numbers on Earth. Historians, notably world or global historians, focus far more explanatory attention on these institutional, movement, and collective *actors* than they do on *spaces* such as cities, despite the essential roles that thick space has played in the largest-scale projects of power deployment. True, cities – even conceived as premier power amplifying and deploying spaces – are never *sufficient* to interpret the historical significance of these actors' projects. But nor are these actors themselves – nor their institutions, their movements, or other collective acts – enough to understand change on their own. To refocus historical interpretation on cities' *essential* role in world history, the pairing of "urban" and "foreland" is quite useful. For urban historians, urban forelands are essential to our field's contribution to global and planetary history.

The names I propose for the four classes of urban forelands – Action, Habitat, Impact, and Consequence – each identify a separate general body of evidence from the past that we can map in space and time to document the extent of the deployment of our power through cities. Each "realm" of urban foreland is its own type of space, but each affects and is affected by all three other realms, again, in necessary if insufficient ways. In history, these four realms vary in size and contain varying densities of the diverse types of evidence that define them – action, habitat, impact, or consequence. All urban forelands also necessarily overlap with urban hinterlands or encompass them. Like all aspects of the Urban Condition, the outer boundaries of urban forelands are blurry, reflecting the graduated nature of the "urban" as well as the ambiguities inherent to the deployment of city-amplified power in time and space.

The history of Realms of Action is the history of spaces specifically occupied by all city-amplified institutional, movement-launched, or other collective projects of human action. Like the history of cities and all other urban forelands, the history of Realms of Action began in many separate birth regions at many birthdates, whenever city-based states or empires, mercantile or profit-making projects, or projects of knowledge production and dissemination, or the disruptive influence of social movements began to reach outward from their birth city and to occupy space beyond. Early city-states and later imperial dynasties often took the lead, conquering and administering other nearby cities and their hinterlands, then using the energy and power available there to reach into realms previously outside the influence of cities, meanwhile also influencing neighboring but previously independent urban birth-regions. Long-distance merchants thickened these large-scale interactions with profit-making projects, and priests and oppositional activists spread their own knowledge and projects of disruption, often using state or commercial infrastructure and vehicles to do so. Migrations and demographic expansions or contractions followed, taking up still other overlapping Realms of Action. Realms of Action can thus add useful specificity to what world historians and global urban historians often somewhat abstractly call "connections" between cities, for these realms often joined several of history's original urban birthplaces into larger Realms of Action – and thus realms of interaction. The space occupied by city-amplified human actions varied in density over space and time, with much more action occurring in cities and nearby, and dispersing outward, affecting thinner and threadlike spaces that doubled as urban hinterlands and then reaching beyond, bringing new thinner and previously non-urban non-city spaces like villages, farms, and camps into the orbit of the Urban Condition to varying degrees. In this way, acts of deploying urban amplified power could extend the ambiguous outer boundary of the Urban Condition even beyond urban hinterlands – or, at other times, cause that boundary to retreat.

The urban forelands that made up Realms of Action coincided with spaces that "world systems" theorists characterize as "cores" and "peripheries" (e.g. Wallerstein, 1974). The relative influence of activities in one urban birth-region over others could give the Urban Condition a "poly-nodal" geography or result in the dominance of a handful of "core" urban regions or even one dominant region over regions that it demotes to peripheries or "semi-peripheries." When our production of cities largely depended on energy harvested in river valleys, cities' forelands of action began to merge in some parts of the world, notably within Southwest Asia, then across the tricontinental interface of the Eastern Mediterranean, eventually also establishing regular ties with South Asia. Cities born in the Huang Ho (Yellow River) Valley meanwhile deployed similarly regular activities throughout China, East Asia, and through Southeast Asia, also reaching to South Asia, there overlapping with eastward flowing actions from the Eastern Mediterranean. By the early Common Era, simultaneous large-scale deployments of action from Rome and Han Dynasty Changan created a vast Realm of Action across the Afro-Asian supercontinent that expanded and retreated over the ensuing millennium, often cementing into a highly interactive multipolar realm of city-amplified activity via monsoon-driven commerce in the Indian Ocean and caravan routes across Central Asia, Arabia, and the Sahara. Similar enlarged Realms of Action connected Mesoamerica, the Mayan Lands of the Yucatan, and urban regions southward toward the Isthmus of Panama. In South America, another Realm of Action encompassed the entirety of the Andean Cordillera (*EP*, chapters 2–5).

Only by tapping energy from the World Ocean after 1500 did the new planet-encompassing urban hinterland allow for the creation of the first Earth-girdling forelands of Action, beginning with the global silver trade after 1571 and increasingly transformed from a polynodal to a unipolar realm of imperial and capitalist practice centered on a succession of European cities ultimately led by London. Urban forelands of Action grew larger and denser, and soon accelerated in both size and density, no longer periodically retreating as they had in premodern times. Realms of Action thus drove what many prefer to call a "process of globalization" that also coincided with one of several important birthdates of a truly planetary Urban Planet. The irregular geography of hydrocarbon deposits like coal mines and oil and gas fields, itself a contingent result of many eons of geological time, in turn at once cemented London's role as a core city in the planetary Realm of Action, then offered more inducements to imperial expansion, then helped explain a catastrophic period of global warfare and urban destruction during the first half of the twentieth century, then encouraged the subsequent shifts of global urban power to multipolar Realms of Action centered in Washington DC, New York, and Moscow, soon supplemented by rival projects of action deployed from Brussels, London, Tokyo, and Beijing. In our time, cities anchor an urban foreland of planetary Action that is far denser and more routine than ever before, thanks in great part to the production – once again in cities – of the technological and physical underpinnings of virtual space (*EP*, chapters 7–10, 13–14, 21–24).

The second type of urban foreland, the Realm of Habitat, represents the space occupied by physical spaces produced by and for humans living under the Urban Condition. Since producing human space requires human action as we know, the Realm of Habitat makes up a sub-province of the Realm of Action, even as the size of that larger realm relies foundationally upon the size of the Realm of Physical Habitat.

In periods where cities grow and multiply, they not only add their own amplified physical built space to the Realm of Habitat but also put tremendous growth pressures on the size of the human habitat consisting of non-cities. The need for new *city-producing* thinner and more threadlike spaces thus acts intrinsically to grow the number and extent of *city-produced* non-city spaces. One large component of the urban foreland of Habitat, in other words, consists of an enlarged urban hinterland itself. Villages and thinner spaces such as farm fields preexisted cities by six millennia or more, but the birth of the urban condition demanded a drastic expansion and a redesign of these thinner spaces to supply growing cities with greater surplus energy harvests. The classic example comes from what is often thought of as the first city, Uruk. The city arose from a village-rich, farm-rich, river valley region, but it immediately demanded a massive redesign of that hinterland. Villages needed to multiply and grow, farms needed to be transformed from small plots into long rectangular fields more suitable for systematic plowing by ox teams, and the river itself needed to be rebuilt to include a vast system of irrigation ditches. These new human spaces can be characterized as non-cities; they remained "rural"; and they were definitively urban hinterlands. But they were also urban forelands of Habitat because their very existence depended on the existence of the city, Uruk itself, and other Sumerian cities nearby. When metalsmiths in one or another of these Sumerian cities invented bronze plowshares, that urban-generated new knowledge too at once demanded and made possible further extensions of this hinterland, in the form of still larger and more efficient farm fields, for example, that did double-duty as part of cities' outward creation of foreland (Liverani, 1998).

As Uruk's governing institutions, social movements, wealth-amassing institutions and knowledge-creating institutions all grew to meet the demands of governing (or disrupting) a city, they too played central roles in these outward deployments of power. Included in their many projects of power deployment were many projects of producing new human habitats, both in the form of new cities and many new non-city spaces (Algaze, 2005). Urban forelands of Habitat thus also grew to include provincial capitals of empires and their offices, diplomatic legations, and monumental architecture, new fortifications and army barracks, new naval bases, but also massive systems of paved roads, gigantic wall systems at imperial frontiers, and archipelagos of dispersed non-city forts. They include the infrastructure of long-distance trade – at a minimum larger and many more mercantile headquarters, courts, mints, customs houses, warehouses, roads, inns, caravanserais, and port facilities, including docks, breakwaters, and lighthouses. Knowledge infrastructure included not only monumental urban temples and processional avenues and squares, but strings of non-city monasteries, shrines, and even isolated libraries, as well as spiritual spaces and schools in thousands of neighborhoods of cities, towns, and villages to transmit new forms of urban knowledge. Shops, markets, and built structures designed for advertising also multiplied in cities and flung themselves outward into countless non-city spaces in the name of producing the commercial knowledge we know as global consumer culture. Social movements, such as those that founded all the major religions we know of today, and later those that expanded the idea of states based on the consent of the governed, could disrupt and repurpose this infrastructure, demand its further redesign, or expand spatial production in cities and far beyond for the movement's own purposes (*EP*, chapters 2–5, 9, 14, etc.).

A final often-ignored component of the Realm of Habitat consists of built structures designed for mobility – vehicles. The bodies of humans and animals were the first to be outfitted for this purpose, but sedan-chairs, carts, carriages, riverboats, and sea-going ships all played decisively important roles not only in the expansion of the urban foreland of Habitat but also in our ability to actually inhabit "extended" space, let alone to harvest increasing inflows of energy from the expanded hinterlands that came into being as a result of our extended habitat. Sailing ships became crucial parts of all seaport urban habitats, but they also served as cities' supreme means of harvesting geo-solar energy from the World Ocean, drastically accelerating the expansion of cities and the increasing globalization of the human habitat after 1500. Harvests of hydrocarbon enabled railroads, asphalt roads, automobiles, trucks, and steamships, military vehicles of all kinds terrestrial, naval, and airborne, and of course passenger airplanes. All these vehicles expanded in number and design, and they demanded and made possible the vast accelerations of city and non-city human space that accompanied successive hydrocarbon energy revolutions. Cars alone must figure as a critical factor in most of the greatly accelerating "extended urbanization" of our own time. Expanding urban peripheries may indeed have been largely generated by "feral" capitalist development, but none of that would be possible if people could not move around within those peripheries at sufficient speed to make them habitable. Threadlike space expanded at even greater rates to accommodate vehicles or to fuel them, including railways, highways, oil and gas pipelines, and electrical wires at the very least. Responding to similar demands, thinner human habitats too were transformed by monumental if often remote non-city energy-producing spaces like coal and metal mines, oil fields, massive dams, and power plants of all kinds (*EP*, chapters 7–8, 14, 19, 24).

Put all these components of the urban foreland of Habitat end-to-end, and you get a city-generated space that swiftly accelerated to planetary scope in the years after the harnessing of energy from the World Ocean. Only after 1900, though, did the thick-plus-thin-plus-threadlike human habitat become a truly planet-encompassing structure, long after the larger Realm of Action. It was then that trans-Pacific telegraph cables completed the contiguous encasement of Earth's surface, marking another birthday of its human-built twin planet, Earthopolis. Since then, these physical manifestations of "extended urbanization," or what natural scientists prefer to call the "anthrome," have not only dramatically increased their grip on our planet, but they have also accelerated the amount of material humans have transferred from Earth's planetary crust into its human one, in the form of wood, stone, brick, asphalt, glass, steel, and above all, fertilizer, plastic, and concrete. Our Urban Planet, in its form as a combined built – or better, terraformed – urban foreland of Habitat, now outweighs the entire ravaged and diminished planetary biosphere upon which our existence depends (*EP*, chapters 14, 24, Elhacham et al., 2020).

Ravaged, indeed. From the very origins of the Urban Condition, the spaces occupied by city-amplified human activities and built habitat have always had far more "extended" effects on the size and shape of extra-human spaces beyond – the Realm of Impact. Of course, we cannot know precisely how big of an impact humanity would have had on our planet if we never built cities. The historical record is clear, however, that once we did begin building them, our impacts on the surface of the Earth diversified, even as they occupied ever greater and denser swaths of space on Earth. This Realm of Impact included our own Habitat, but also spaces where we did not act or live, not only across the two dimensions of our planet's hard and watery surface but below and above its surface as well, impacting Earth's life-giving relationship to the Sun.

The history of the Realm of Impact is a crucial part of the story about how humans used our cities to first audition for and then take a leading role alongside much older geophysical and biological forces in the business of transforming planetary history – that is, in bending Earth Time. The actions we took to build cities, encompassed as we know by broad categories of production, amplifica-tion, and deployment, amounted to an extension of our existential gamble that we could use our spatially amplified power to "clutch" more from the Holocene

Epoch's relatively generous and stable supply of natural energy and thus minimize our vulnerability to the times when that energy supply pulsed violently upward or downward nonetheless. As in all human gambles, we placed our bets on cities without perfect information and thus at great risk. As inhabitants of cities powered mostly by rivers, our biggest risks and impacts came from the impact of our failed gambles on our own terraformation of river valleys. Channeling river water into irrigation ditches, for example, may have led to soil salinization and other forms of degradation, likely cutting off the energy harvestable in the Tigris and Euphrates rivers after 500 BCE. Felling trees for fuel, building materials, or to open new city-feeding cropland caused silt to build up on river bottoms, raising their level and causing city-destroying floods. That forced us to construct ever higher retaining structures, and in China, caused the Yellow River to radically change the location of its delta several times over the course of global urban history. All of this, of course, occurred as the ebbs and flows of Holocene Epoch's geophysical and biological energy production retained the upper hand in determining all the biggest threats to our existence: floods, droughts, storms, mudslides, siltation, and ebbs and flows of forestland.

Still, humans' city-amplified "endogenous" Impacts exacerbated "exogenous" downturns unlike ever before. Somewhat lighter impacts came from burning wood, charcoal, and small amounts of coal, notably in the case of Roman- and Han-era metal mining and smelting when plumes of toxic ash and smoke left traces on Greenland's ice sheets, suggesting our species' first city-enabled invasion of the planetary atmosphere. Rice paddies, which humans expanded dramatically to meet the needs of East Asian cities, involved prodigious outflows of methane from the lithosphere and hydrosphere into the atmosphere. Some paleoclimatologists believe that these greenhouse gas emissions may have acted to stabilize Holocenic energy cycles. If so, these premodern impacts constituted our first audition in city-enabled global warming – and the Realm of Impact became the first of our urban forelands to reach planetary scope (*EP*, chapter 6; Ruddiman, 2014; Brooke, 2014).

These impacts accelerated when we used our cities to harvest vast new inputs of energy from the World Ocean and later fossilized sunshine. Impacts like deforestation and transformed rivers spread to all continents and most major river valleys. As new global empires encouraged the ascendancy of carbon capitalism, pollution from burning wood and other biomass expanded and dangerous coal smoke pollution accelerated. Methane invasions of the atmosphere grew dramatically and were joined by radically accelerating invasions by carbon dioxide, nitrous oxide, sulfur dioxide, aerosols, particulates, and microplastics. Mining operations diversified, spread, and mushroomed in size, leaching larger outflows of poison downriver and into soils. The chemistry of the

Earth's surface diversified as we fed our growing billions by inventing, then spreading farm fields with fertilizers, pesticides, herbicides, and the increasingly elaborate industrial compounds that made them up; river bottoms absorbed these chemicals in particularly high doses, then sent them into oceanic dead zones around their deltas. Groundwater supplies required for bioengineered crops depleted, shifting the massive weight of our planet's hydrosphere toward the oceans, thus even possibly affecting the tilt of Earth's axis. Cities themselves, as our great sites of enlargement and concentration, absorbed all of these energies and substances in ever more massive quantities: in building materials like steel, glass, and concrete that all required enormous acts of carbon-burning; in electric power heavily derived from coal; in interior heating and home cooking energy supplied by petroleum and methane; and in disposable household and industrial goods increasingly made of petroleum-derived plastic or packaged in it.

In the early twenty-first century, when our Realm of Habitat began to outweigh that of the extra-human biosphere, it was also in part because we had simultaneously diminished the weight of Earth's living things, notably by chopping down trees or burning rainforest lands, adding their mass to that of our buildings or to the megatons of carbon in the overloaded atmosphere. Vehicles, our habitats of movement within cities and throughout the increasingly dense threadlike spaces of transport infrastructure, also became petroleum-driven, thus adding their own vast realm of carbon impact. Outflows of urban waste, once dominated by our own excrement and food waste, also accelerated, accumulating in enormous dumps of non-biodegradable human-made materials on land, in floating debris in rivers and in ocean gyres, in addition to accounting for a disproportionate share of emissions into our radically heating atmosphere. Vast inequalities within and between the Global North and the Global South, meanwhile, guaranteed that all these Urban Planet-defining Impacts fell hardest on those who did the least to set them in motion. Accumulators of capital, notably anyone who creates profit from the financing, mining, and combustion of carbon, and the imperial states that brokered the rise of the global landscapes of coal, gas and above all petroleum extraction bear the biggest blame, as theoreticians who coined the term "Capitalocene" rightly claim. However, the increased reliance on carbon burning for basic human domestic, work, and consumer life, notably in the Global North but also increasingly in many Global South locations, implicates "Us" all, if by a range of far smaller degrees to be sure (*EP*, chapters 9, 14, 24).

All that leaves historians to calculate highly contradictory, if increasingly grim, Consequences of our 6,000-year gamble with the Urban Condition, as measured in the amount of life we created in space on Earth – human and extra-human. These Consequences too occupy a spatial realm, usefully under-stood as a fourth type of urban foreland. To theorize and historicize this Realm of Consequence most usefully, we can map it onto our planet's many remark-able ecosystems – propelled as they are by their own multifarious symbioses of life and death – and onto Earth's biosphere as a whole.

Cities, of course, are biological ecosystems themselves, and under the rules of our gamble on the Urban Condition, their own production of life and death regularly served as the mile-zero-posts for all human-made Realms of Consequence. As ecosystems, cities are so dominated by our own species that our own highly unequal interactions with each other – comprised by the deep contingencies of our acts of power deployment that make up the *polis* of Earthopolis – determine much in terms of their calculus of life and death. Any "symbioses" that exist within human ecosystems on their own are highly prone to destabilization by violence, war, inequality, enslavement, poverty, and invidi-ous differentiations by culture, gender, and body-type. Thus, our own deploy-ments of urban power are responsible for many of the most negative consequences of our own bets on city-amplified deployments of power upon the size and the well-being of our own species – a "biopolitics" that often collapses into "necropolitics." Human cruelty to other humans played a central role in all of the many periods of "collapse" and high self-inflicted death-dealing that punctuated the history of cities of the rivers, even if Holocenic energy downswings often played a role. Similar dynamics continued under the city-amplifying auspices of the World Ocean and hydrocarbon, especially as both new forms of energy helped us deploy ever more destructive forms of gunpow-der, and then atomic weaponry. The imperial bloodletting of 1914 to 1945 resulted in more destruction of cities and the Realm of Habitat than ever before, along with the loss of over 100 million human lives. Though early modern and modern warfare never led to prolonged periods of collapse, there is no reason to believe that we could not repeat these feats in the near future, especially given the destabilized geo-solar energy flows – and disinformation flows – of Our Time (*EP*, chapters 6, 9, 21, 25).

Other than ourselves, we also share cities – not to mention the non-city stretches of the Urban Condition – with animals, plants, fungi, and microbiota essential to all of each other's cycles of life and death. Large, domesticated animals and prodigious amounts of plant life have continually provided labor, movement, air and water quality, temperature modulation, storm protection, disease immunity, knowledge, and above all food, without which there would be no human species, let alone no cities or any Urban Condition. Yet cities, assisted by their existential connections to non-city urban space, also amount to an enormous eco-systemic incubator of life for humanity's greatest killers, the pathogenic bacteria, viruses, yeasts, and molds that regularly pass from non-human to human reservoirs, often at the thinnest, blurriest boundary of the Urban Condition, and accelerate in the concentrated vortexes of juxtaposed human hosts (and other animals and plant hosts) these species can find in thicker spaces, emerging as wholesale dealers in human misery and death. Once again, upward and downward swings of geo-solar energy could favor or retard these life-giving-and-life-taking Consequences of human-built ecosystems and the space they occupy. Technologies of air, water, and waste-flow, within and outside cities, also mattered. So did systems of scientific knowledge production and dissemination and health-creating facilities like schools, clinics, hospitals, and universities, all of which went through enormous accelerations of their own at various points in global urban history. Cities, assisted by their mass mobilization of equally disease-prone armies, gave us the most catastrophic episodes of lost human life in history: thousands of plagues and epidemics, topped off by the Antonine and Justinian plagues, the Black Death, the devastating invasions of the Americas by Afro-Eurasian disease strains of all kinds in the sixteenth century, the scourges that followed again afterward worldwide, the cholera epidemics and other ills of the nineteenth century, the plague and the influenza epidemics of the early twentieth century, and the mounting viral epidemics of the last seventy-five years, topped by AIDS and COVID-19. The geographies of these scourges help us trace deathly flares of the Realm of Consequence from super-continental to planetary dimensions, marking still other birthdays of Earthopolis.

That said, thus far, the life-giving potential of our bet with the Urban Condition has paid off as far as human life is concerned. Whenever cities' intakes of food, water, air, energy, and fuel grew along with the size and efficiency of urban hinterlands, they enabled massive collective bursts in human reproduction, including the doubling of our global population during the various Bronze Ages, Iron Ages, "Classic" Ages, "Golden" and "High" Ages of the ninth through fourteenth centuries, and the Oceanic Age from 1500 to 1800. Each of those periods also increased the size of cities themselves, including the number of million-plus cities beginning with Rome and escalated during subsequent periods of human population doubling. During the age of hydrocarbon, when urban ecosystems were outfitted with new public health amenities that diminished infant mortality and adult misery and dramatically increased life expectancy, the human population doubled at an increasing rate, forming the upward swing of the J-Curves that represent the Greatest Acceleration of Our Time. City growth passed all bounds, passing 5, 10, and 30 million people in a growing number of places. Some cities are now projected to house 50–80 million by the twenty-first century's end. The most consequential of all Realms of Consequence is the increasingly dense – if still thin, thick, and threadlike – space that 8 billion living humans occupy on Earth (*EP*, chapters 6, 9, 21, 25).

Yet accelerating Realms of human (and microbiotic) life also spread Consequences of a far grimmer kind, an unequally-and-oppositely accelerating Realm of Death for thousands of other plant and animal species. From the time we first domesticated animals and plants, if not before, we have grown used to playing God with planetary biology, creating life-forms that were more obedient and useful to us and disfavoring those that did not meet our needs, or that we needed so greedily as to kill off, or that stood in the way of one or another of our most grandiose gambles with human power. Cities allowed us to accelerate this business, diminishing biodiversity of all kinds, starting with the enormous advantage we granted to domesticated livestock, commercial poultry, and monocrops over other species in our own day. In the twilight of the Holocene, all of these human-encouraged and human-redesigned species far outnumber – and outweigh – all other wild animal and plant species combined, and by a wide margin. In the meantime, our global "Great Hunts," first set off by the discovery of the World Ocean, killed off billions of animals for their skins, feathers, fuel oil, and edible flesh. We extinguished ecosystem-anchoring apex predators for the dangers they provided to livestock, and in the case of the plains Buffalo, committed ecocide to deprive Native Americans of a once abundant source of food to weaken their resistance to European settlers. Meanwhile, our trans-oceanic translocations of plants and animals introduced invasive species that have destabilized many millennia-old local ecosystems. Among the many consequences that the Age of Humans will impose on the planetary fossil record is a record number of species that, like us, inhabit Earth as a whole, and which, like us, threaten extinction to many other species – thus guaranteeing their disappearance from fossil records of future Epochs. Biologists routinely compare the destruction of ecosystems caused by invasives and our destruction of non-human habitat to the consequences of an asteroid colliding with Earth. If geophysical forces like collisions between rocks and planets explain the five earlier great extinctions we can detect in fossil records, Our Urban Planet, humanity's current choice of ecosystem, appears for the first time in Earth Time to have amplified the power of a singularly destructive biological species – us – to bring about a sixth (*EP*, chapters 21, 25; Thomas, 2022).

Proposition 6: Polyrhythmic Plotlines – Urban Temporality

Cities matter not just to space but to time. How, exactly? As the time-specialists in the urban studies room, surely urban historians can contribute to theories of urban temporality. A definition of the city that rests on boxes of verbs like To Produce, To Amplify, and To Deploy helps. Theories of time ideally characterize the shape of change, its periodization, its occupation of space, and the patterns of causality – injections of power into time – that animate change. Cities, I propose, gave us more power to bend time – and in more ways at once – than we possessed before. The result was not the invention of history itself, as we once theorized, but a more diverse temporal counterpoint, filled with more simultaneous melodic shapes, time signatures, and rhythms all proceeding at multiple tempos at once, from the very small and acute to the most thrumming and enormous – all guided by our own city-diversified, juxtaposed, amplified, and colliding projects of power. Only a theory of urban temporality that starts with the polyrhythmic pulses of projects of power deployment can handle their most minute and predictably unpredictable historical traces while also pacing urban planetary time alongside the much deeper drumbeats of Earth Time.

Theories of "civilization" – the old word for the Urban Condition – once held that time stood still until we invented cities. At that point, prehistory, characterized either by timelessness or at least a lack of meaningful change, gave way to history, or at least the history of states, of capital and money, and/or of writing and "real" knowledge – the kind of knowledge that was recorded in sufficient clarity and surviving quantity to be worthy of study by professional "historians." Archeologists and paleoanthropologists have since consigned the conceit of "prehistory" to the waste-bin of history, and "deep historians" have confirmed the error. Cultural theorists nailed the coffin shut, noting the resemblance of such binary "pre- and post-" temporal theories to those flogged by racists and orientalists, including theories that invidiously compared the time-dynamic "Modern Cities" of the West to the supposedly still-timeless "Old Cairos" or "Old Delhis" that imperial officials happily demoted to monuments of a changeless past (*EP*, chapter 13).

The idea that cities transformed human time from a more homogeneous, even perhaps more predictable, phenomenon into a far more jangling polyrhythmic one risks similar invidiousness. If so, I am fully prepared to accept that verdict. We now know that people living in non-cities before there were cities (or outside the influence of cities after that) have left behind evidence of a deeply complex sense of time, including highly sophisticated sensitivities to relationships between human, planetary, lunar, and solar time. The power that non-city dwellers deployed through their polities took polyrhythmic patterns too, and scholars who study such matters can no doubt shed light on ways to compare these deeper patterns of change with the "even-more-polyrhythmic" patterns that I propose for the Urban Condition. Indeed, the polyrhythmic nature of urban time I propose here must remain flexible enough to encompass a perfectly valid opposing claim, that Our Urban Planet has made humanity far *more timeless* than at any point in the history of human condition, Urban or otherwise. The acceleration of cities and of urban planetary growth, after all, is coterminous with the extinction of temporal diversity – the disappearance of once highly-varied timepieces, clocks, calendars, and numeration systems to mark the years and centuries. Railroad companies brought a universal system of time zones to Earthopolis; imperial capitalism unified us around the Julio-Christian calendar with its twelve strangely-shaped months, its leap-years, its zero-year, and its "common" and "before common" era designations; and atomic clocks strive to use the same exact sweep of hours, minutes, and seconds to dictate the daytimes of all humans (or at least all of us who own a digital timepiece). For a theory of polyrhythmic time to hold, we must treat the very real homogenization of time as one powerful melodic line – but only one – in the otherwise ever-more jangled, tune-filled, multiply time-signatured, unmeasured, and perhaps unmeasurable counterpoint that urban planetary time has in fact become (compare Koselleck, 2018).

How so? If there is indeed a distinct *urban* temporality, my proposal for its theorization starts with the city-making practices To Produce, To Amplify, and To Deploy. Most verbs contain a temporal dimension, and each of these boxes contains acts that, as they produce space and power, also occur in time, shape time, and help explain time. They occur *in time* in that earlier history always matters – both in William Faulkner's famous sense that "the past is never dead" and "is not even past," but also in the sense that other, earlier projects of power deployment, especially the most powerful ones that most affected previous space and time, always provide political, economic, cultural, or demographic contexts (sometimes called "path dependencies") within which new ones must be enacted. The energy of the Sun and Earth, of course, provide other, "environmental" contexts. That said, new projects, especially ones whose deployment involves especially large amounts of power, also contain the potential to *shape* time, including Earth Time. Some projects demonstrate that power by creating "continuities" – that is the power to successfully advance their purpose over long periods without major change brought on by rival projects or environmental changes. Others demonstrate their power by "disruption" of otherwise longstanding continuities and by causing abrupt breaks or changes in time. For historians, evidence of continuity in various dimensions, and evidence of change of various levels of disruptive power always coexist, guaranteeing some level of temporal counterpoint that requires both descriptive and explanatory interpretation. In recent years, theorists have called such coexisting temporalities "layered" time, "durabilities," "sediments," or temporal "hauntings" (e.g. Gordon, 2008; Stoler, 2016; Koselleck, 2018).

In cities, I propose, counterpoints of temporal continuity and change are far more likely to take especially complex, "layered" or, as I prefer to call them, polyrhythmic forms. In part, this is because cities are produced by – and are far more likely to produce – projects enacted in the context of diversification, juxtaposition, and catalysis. More importantly, though, it is because subsequent acts of power deployment in cities are characterized by so many possibilities of action as to be predictably unpredictable. Not only do cities, in other words, harbor so many more efforts to shape time in one space at any given time, but the interactions of urban projects – whether guided by alignment, differentiation, conflict, negotiation, appropriation, distribution, disruption, or governance – contain far more potential for what we might call "causal pileups" that will not only strain descriptive analyses of continuity and change, but also challenge historians' explanatory analyses by virtue of the sheer number of time-shaping factors that pile up. These causal pileups sometimes result in surprise changes that can be especially difficult to explain given the multiplicity of factors at play – a form of time often rendered by the name "contingency." But the absence of change should also probably surprise historians more often than it does, for sometimes continuity seems – or should seem – equally inexplicable, given the existence of multiplying possibilities for countervailing projects intent on change, especially in cities. In this instance, I have used my "theory by verb" to infer the existence, in cities, of multiplying causal pileups that strain both descriptive and explanatory interpretation. However, I am convinced that historians spending any day professionally immersed in archive boxes filled with vestiges of the urban past – that is, who are behaving primarily like empiricists rather than theoreticians – will be hard-pressed to characterize the times they discover there in any other way.

If I am right about the polyrhythmic nature of urban temporality, I think theorists and historians ought to revisit our near addiction to the temporal and causal concept "process." Urban historians do not typically scrutinize concepts we borrow wholesale from theory, but it is easy enough to see that "process" has, in the absence of alternatives, filled an urgent need for complex under-standings of both space and time – "urban" and "history" no less. In the case of space, we use "urban processes" or "urbanization" to signal that cities are not just hard "things" – "static" assemblages of structures – but "dynamic" spaces inhabited by actual people who, over time, are always changing those spaces, how they live in them, and how they think about doing so. In the case of time, we use "process" to explain transformations in time with complex or even dialect-ical causalities that have particularly pronounced or continuous historical con-sequences in the historical record. Typically, a "process" is a continuous arc of change that is supported by powerful actors whose interests are served by the change, but who may, individually, possess little power to alter the direction of that arc once it is set "in process." "Processes of capitalist urbanization" are a classic example of such concepts, though "state formation," imperialism, colonization, decolonization, modernization (or modernity), civilization, and globalization, not to mention planetary urbanization itself, all identify highly complex long-term temporal changes whose driving mix of causalities we typically analyze with the temporal abbreviation "process."

My problem with "process" is not so much what it seeks to do (that is, add dynamism and complexity to temporal analysis), but that it does so by shearing actors, actions, purposes, and their power out of our conclusions about change. Relying on process as an abbreviation for change erases the *who?* the *how?* and a big portion of the *why?* from time, not to mention the beating heart of history – urban and otherwise – the verbs themselves. Indeed, "process" explains historical change unsatisfactorily in the passive voice. The same is true when we further embalm processes not as verbs, but as gerunds – most importantly by fitting spatial adjectives like "urban" or "global" with the suffix "-ization."

On top of that, "process" cannot shake the stench of its mono-directional cognate "procession." It thus bears mixed messages about the very complexities of temporality we hope to communicate by using the term. "Urbanization" and "globalization" do no better: They cannot avoid insinuating that time only goes in one direction, impervious to the contingencies that riddle the history of cities and the globe, including the big ones we face today. Most theorists of process, to be sure, try to obviate that problem: Their "processes," they insist, are "dialectical," "highly contingent," and "multicausal." The fact that the "process of capitalist urbanization," in its classic formulations (e.g. Harvey, 1989) includes its own "crises" and "spatial fixes" suggests as much. Most theorists of process also avoid the trap of the most simplistic unidirectional "concentration effects" theorists, or theorists who cut off possibilities for change at a given historical moment by asserting the weight of "path dependencies" previously set in stone. If our intention is to assert the complexity of time, though, why embalm it in concepts that wash temporal polyrhythms and causal multiplicities into abstraction, or worse, offer a depersonalized, mechanized, unidirectional, "presentist," or even teleological rendition of time?

In searching for alternate nouns to express polyrhythmic urban temporality, I much prefer "project." As a concept of change, project refocuses causal analysis on historical actors themselves, on the choices they make to concatenate acts of space and power production, the purposes and "agency" behind those choices, and the many contingencies built into the deployment of their projects alongside others at the same time. "Project" allows the interpretation of polyrhythmic time to proceed in the active voice. With projects, we enter the business of human time-making at its moment of conception and first impact rather than somewhere in the middle of the ensuing consequences, or worse, from some "resolved" far end looking backward. Project also allows us to interpret human time at its molecular level – akin to a musicologist examining a single musical gesture, or a critic examining a nuance of style at the level of syntax or sentence structure. Indeed, we can see projects as the basic element of time's otherwise multiplying rhythms, melodies, and colliding plotlines. The basic form of a project, after all, is that of all human stories: "Someone (people, main character) somewhere (space, setting) wanted (purpose, motivation) so they acted (put their power or agency into practice), but (conflict or contingency: drama), and so they . . . (the plot twists disruptively, the denouement sets in – or perhaps continuity resets itself, if never 'happily forever after')."

More than restoring access to time's active voice, "projects" also allow us to revisit dialectics that connect between the smallest, most situated enactments of human purpose and power with those that play out on larger scales, while keeping us far more accountable for the possibility of any analytic erasures along the way. The search for projects thus ensures epistemological humility even as the polyrhythmic thrum we observe in our archives gathers in complexity, conflict, compromise, "turbulence," and waning theorizability; even as likely unequal increases in the amount of power available to various projects result in enormous inequalities of cause and effect; and thus even as the smallest things – occasionally, often contingently – become enormous, "worlding," or even planetary things.

Projects of time-making based on projects of space and power also give us access to the molecular structure of spatiotemporal downscaling and upscaling. Faced with Charles Tilly's admonition to link local and global "processes," urban historians should start by breaking up "process" itself, along with other abstract temporalities. Instead, reimagine our field of study planted with projects of space–power production, amplification, and deployment. Watch as these efforts intersect dialectically with larger-scale institutional, movement-propelled, or other collective projects of action, creating "diascalar" or "transpatialized" dynamics (Nightingale, 2015; Schayegh, 2017). Projects to "form a state," to "accumulate capital," to disseminate new knowledge, to transfer power to a sovereignty-seeking movement all retain their internal conflicts. Their crises become not part of a "process," a story whose ending we already know, but contingent on the polymorphic dialectics that accompany all efforts to deploy space and power – once again including all acts of alignment and differentiation, negotiation and conflict, appropriation and distribution, narrative and counter-narrative, governance and disruption.

Projects, we should be clear, tend to center what we conventionally call "political" causality. If so, they highlight the widest sense of that word, the sense that critical theorists embrace when they rename their various fields "political economy," "cultural politics," "racial" or "gender politics," "infra-politics," "biopolitics," or "political ecology" – precisely to highlight the impact of power-negotiating forces and institutions on their subject of analysis. Not only does the concept of project allow for a better transfer of analysis between these otherwise siloed fields, it is also useful for re-centering the spatial, and thus the urban, in them all. The English word for "politics" and "city" famously share the Greek root *polis* – with the added benefits that the original concept *polis* also included cities' hinterlands and signaled that the "politics" in the *polis* is in some way distinct from that in non-cities alone.

Linking human *polis* to Earth, the main mission of a historical theory of Our Urban Planet, also benefits from time construed in terms of polyrhythmic consequences of projects immersed in these dialectics of spatial downscaling and upscaling. Our basic existential gambles with city-amplified harvests of geo-solar energy, after all, took the basic form of spatiotemporal political projects that led to their own polyrhythmic combinations of continuity, contingency, and disruption – including the long transformations in urban time represented by cities of the rivers, oceans, and hydrocarbon. It is even worth thinking of the Holocene Epoch itself in analogous terms, for though it was not a product of human projects, it came into being as an uncanny, highly contingent succession of bends in Earth Time that turned out to be remarkably humano-philic. The mild oscillations of geo-solar energy that characterize the Holocene constitute what may be called an 11,700-year continuity made up of irregular and unprecedented interactions between the Sun's own uneven cycles of high and low power, variable ongoing expansions and contractions of Earth's orbit, the unpredictably changing tilt of our planetary axis, and a period of relatively mild iterations of tectonic and volcanic events on Earth. The fact that the various geophysical oscillations that govern these phenomena lined up the way they did, especially given their far more volatile habit over most of Earth Time, then somehow repeated the production of "Goldilocks" conditions over twelve millennia, should figure as one of the biggest surprises – even miracles – in all Earth Time (Zalasiewicz and Williams, 2012; Brooke, 2014).

From those observations, it is useful to offer a final summation of the longest time spans of human city-based projects of power deployment alongside the human-friendly time swings of the Sun and Earth of the Holocene Epoch. Our first projects of harvesting city-making energy from rivers (and other rain-fed water-based hinterlands) allowed us to build cities, super-continental urban forelands of Action, and large and often interconnected but regional Realms of Habitat, while setting in motion sparse but truly planetary Realms of Impact and super-continental flares of forelands of Consequence, notably during urban-amplified pandemics. Measured in terms of the extent of these urban spaces, however, and in the ebbing and flowing size of the human population, the first 5,500 years of urban history were a story of expansion, retreat (sometimes even collapse), and incrementally greater expansion registered in at least four long episodes of human population doubling mentioned earlier – during the Bronze and Iron Ages, the Classic Age, and the High or Golden Ages from about 800 to 1350. Despite intervening years of regional retreat, humans were able to reproduce our total numbers to about 400 million by the end of the fourth of these more propitious Holocenic "Optimums." If we accept climate historian John L. Brookes's argument that these rises and falls correspond roughly to the "Goldilocks" cycles of the first-ever city-enabling Epoch in Earth Time, we can say that the Cities of the Rivers endowed the Urban Condition with a *syn-Holocenic* temporality.

The polyrhythms of urban time changed in important ways once we began new projects of fueling our cities with far greater harvests of energy from the planet-encompassing hinterland of the World Ocean. Our urban forelands of Action grew to planetary dimensions, while our Realm of Habitat expanded as hundreds of new cities and their hinterlands came into being on all six continents. Our already planetary Realm of Impact became denser, and our Realm of Deathly Consequence too became multicontinental – as disease pandemics that were somewhat under control in Afro-Eurasian cities devastated those in the Americas and Australasia. The transition to Cities of the World Ocean, however, coincided with the Holocene's worst energy downturn, the "Little Ice Age," whose various sub-cycles caused disease, famine, exacerbated warfare, and the deaths of possibly hundreds of millions. That climate downswing did not end until about 1850. Still, despite its miseries, by 1800 the human population had doubled once again – and the Urban Condition had taken the unmistakable dimensions of Our Urban Planet. During the early modern period, thanks to the new Earth-wide gamble we made on cities, we inhabited a new form of temporality that could be considered *counter-Holocenic*.

The story that followed is familiar enough. Cities that were fueled increasingly from the planet's highly dispersed minable hinterlands of various hydrocarbon fuels allowed our urban forelands of Action, Habitat, Impact, and Consequence to grow and thicken explosively, accelerating the impact of the Urban Condition everywhere on the planet. Earth was twinned with Earthopolis – a planetary doppelganger as much created by the polyrhythmic thrumming of human power projects of all kinds as it was by the Holocene's remaining gasps of "Goldilocks"-style energy production. The underworldly gamble with fossil fuel – above all a project of empire, capital, racial supremacy, and patriarchal attitude toward nature – led to the human-led redesign of Earth's atmosphere as a heat-trapping planetary greenhouse. Planetary heating lies at the forefront of many-pronged transformations inaugurating exactly what Earth Systems scientists have proposed: an *anti-Holocenic* form of urban temporality, one that has likely consigned miraculous not-too-hot-not-too-cold polyrhythms of natural energy to the geological past. Humanity will need to find a way to survive in hotter and harsher conditions – while deepening the dialectical connection between the space of consummate human power – "Earthopolis," Our Urban Planet – and the dawn of Our Epoch in Earth Time.

Proposition 7: Morality Tales, Visions, and Miracles – Urban Futures

Some things we can know about cities, and some things maybe we can't – the urban future least of all. Cities remain a leap of faith, as they were when we first gambled on the power that they gave us. Does a history-based theory of Our Urban Planet provide even a threadbare view of what is to come – a diagnosis, say, that could result in a cure? Old morality tales about the virtues or depravity of cities do little to predict the future of an Urban Planet made up of the interactions of city and non-city spaces whose capacities to generate life and death are as internally varied as they are different from each other. Nor, knowing about the polyrhythmic temporality of Our Urban Planet, should we embrace top-down tales of a perfect future when Earthopolis becomes truly "anti-Anthropocenic" without conflict. We are left with the power of projects of human action, in space and time. As Hannah Arendt, the great philosopher of power, counseled us in all matters of the human condition, these collective projects must be conceived in the active voice; they must begin again and again at each moment of the present. They must be visionary. But they will always be contested, and they will always involve leaps of faith. And they will always produce occasional miracles – both very small and very large.

Urban theory is as old as urban history, and both are as old as urban prognostication. Six millennia ago, at Uruk, the Sumerians divined the future in the past in at least three ways that are still with us. They told morality tales about the city and the country. They plotted out ideal godlike cities of the future. And they produced theories that more honestly confronted the basic uncertainties of our species' gamble on the Urban Condition.

When the Sumerians wrote morality tales, they tended to exalt cities. This they did by means of the "Holy *Mē*," a metaphysical concept sometimes translated as the "Arts of Civilization" (Wolkenstein and Kramer, 1983), but that could just as easily stand in for "a theory of the Urban Condition." In these tales, cities were the vessels of all that was true, just, divinely inspired, refined, pious, experimental, innovative, exciting, and at the cutting edge of carnal desire. On the flipside of the enlightened city was the figure of the bumbling, rustic villager – and more tellingly, the specter of the raw nomad. Their rudimentary villages, hovels, tents, clothes, food, governments, knowledge, religions, and sexual practices invited extreme condescension, laced with fear. City chauvinism surfaced in all subsequent birthplaces of cities, adding, varying, and remixing urban spatial virtues over time, while dominating the history of urban theory and becoming a foundational component of the Urban Condition itself. No doubt these accumulating tales of wonderment help explain why so many of us give up our lifetimes to studying cities today. Yet, counter-narratives trailed these narratives wherever they emerged, also becoming one with the Urban Condition. In these, cities were morally and politically corrupting or softening, too chaotic for contemplative thought or piety, spaces of unbridled greed, dirt, noise, chaos, anomie, and violence, the perfect vessels for tyranny – not to mention humanity's greatest weapon in our war against nature. In these counter-morality tales, villages, farms, and pastures became separate and opposite Arcadias – the only possible site for common-sense government, holiness, face-to-face honesty, incorruptibility, independence, relief, peace, and clarity, not to mention seats of humanity's noblest stewardship of Earth.

As ancient and enduring as this narrative/counter-narrative duet may be, it has no useful place in predicting the urban futures of our day. "City mice" and "country mice" are co-citizens of our singular urban planetary polity, composed of a quasi-infinite plurality of both city and non-city components. Some of these spaces contribute more to all life on Earth, some contribute to more death, but neither city nor non-city offers any life-form, human or otherwise, any undifferentiated claim to a moral higher ground. This has been true ever since we cast our lot with thicker spaces connected to thinner ones by more threadlike ones. In that way, the urban future is indeed "dependent" on a hard "path" set in the past. We will only make a better future by better acts within – and in between – all the component parts of Our Urban Planet.

Some Sumerians foresaw this problem. They told the urban future a second way, through tales of the ideal, unconflicted urban society. In or around the year 3200 BCE, an urban theorist on the ziggurat of Uruk carved this kind of perfect vision of the Urban Condition onto the smooth alabaster sides of a beautiful object we know as the Warka Vase. The crucial feature of the story was a wavy line carved at the very bottom of the vase, visually supporting everything above: the mighty, city-making Euphrates River. Just above that, in the lowermost of three carved friezes, an abundant urban hinterland bulges with grain fields, date orchards, gamboling sheep, and lowing oxen. In the middle frieze further up, the people of Uruk dutifully convey the bounty of Earth and Sun in a unidirectional procession toward the temple of their goddess, the mighty Inanna. On the topmost frieze of the vase is Inanna herself. Blessing the offerings, she instructs her attendants to store the city's riches in her temple for redistribution at her divine instruction.

Like many perfect-city stories from ensuing millennia, the Warka Vase reorients the story of the Holy *Mē*. The city-country competition melts into a tale about an idealized relationship between all human spaces and Earth. Each component of the Urban Condition has found its rightful place. The inhabitants are all portrayed unclothed and fully aligned in their devotion to Inanna, as if literally stripped of all self-interest. Governance, accumulation, and devotion – that is, politics, economics, and culture – meld into one another. Conflict, let alone urban "turbulence," is nonexistent. Finally, as the Warka Vase makes plainly clear, all of this came into being from the topmost frieze down. After all, what could better convey a city toward perfection than divine power, wealth, and wisdom?

As I hope my propositions suggest, I find this age-old genre of urban prognostication highly unreliable too. On the one hand, I applaud the comfort with which the theorist of Uruk contemplates the "bigger picture." I also believe in lofty visions; no doubt a propitious future for Our Urban Planet will, like Inanna's, rely to some extent on the power of states, concentrations of wealth, and widely shared cultures of devotion. The problem is the willingness to use theory to erase the least theorizable aspects of urban space, urban time, and the power that drives urban action – and to do so, as in the case of the Vase, in service to the propaganda of a powerful priestly elite. In thousands of dynastic river-capitals that followed, visions of faultless, heaven-anointed urban futures likewise served iron-fisted monarchs and emperors at the expense of much more hopeful alternatives. In 1492, Christopher Columbus's vision of fortress cities along far ocean shores devoted to Glory, Gold, and God launched a hundred European imperial scrambles, erasing alternative relationships between humans and Earth. Capitalist financial centers in a few anointed cities supported these scrambles, as did dungeons and slaving ships along the African coast and a vast archipelago of slave plantations and seaports in the Americas. Hydrocarbon later brought out the worst in these visions, for the comparative power that fossil fuel gave to cities of what we later called the Global North encouraged a glorification of a permanent human exploitation of nature with little concern for its spreading Realms of Consequence. Taken up wholesale by nineteenth- and twentieth-century imperial states, capitalists, and the avatars of a global consumer culture, visions of the urban future like this gave comfort to the entire "intersectional" pantheon of urban archvillains that Kanishka Goonewardena exposed in his essay on totality; it is these very same city-power-appropriators that theorists of the Anthropocene correctly expose as the primary planet-pillagers of Our Time. Among their many crimes were their attempts to seize a monopoly on the production of legitimate urban knowledge. Much like the temple theorist of the Warka Vase, they smothered plurality in nakedly self-interested singularities of a state, of capital, of "markets," of a dominant race, gender, nation, or religion. Along the way, such ideal visions rejiggered the components of the Urban Condition, leaving behind a mechanical interlock of gears, springs, whistles, and beeps – the whole thing encased in a timepiece that ticked off stepwise moments in a one-way ascendant future designed to ring out triumphantly at the endpoint of all time. This is the type of totality that no urban theory, historical or otherwise, should use to foresee any but the most apocalyptic of urban futures. In her intervention into the planetary urbanization debate, the theorist Kate Derrickson rightly calls out such supreme arrogance for what it is: a "god trick" (Derrickson, 2018).

Skepticism about such tricks existed in Sumer too. Some Sumerians ventured a third way to translate theory into prophecy by humbling divine vision itself. A good example is the myth of Inanna and the riverboat, a series of cuneiform texts recovered from fragments of clay tablets, likely the work of multiple residents of the city. These texts reveal Inanna in the full fierceness of her split-persona of creator and destroyer. Conflict permeates the story from the beginning when she must use guile to steal the Holy *Mē* from her father, the god of the rivers. Then she fends off a series of raging calamities that he launches her way as she ferries the goods up the Euphrates on a riverboat. Finally, she herself raises a vast flood in the streets of Uruk to speed her arrival at the city's docks, where she hastily tosses the *Mē* into the hands of the people before the river can take them back. And what a chaotic collection her components of cityhood turn out to be! Certainly, state officials of all kinds splay the docks: kings, queens, priests, and priestesses, along with all their official regalia, weapons, and propaganda. Urban refinements are jumbled there too, in piety, all the arts, food, and lovemaking, not to mention the "the stable home" and "family procreation." But the Uruk of the riverboat myth is as plural and contentious as it is transcendent. Far from the homogenized devotees on the Warka Vase, the riverboat delivers specialties of every sort to the people of Uruk, each with their own interest to pursue. Also tossed about on the docks is a long list of volatile verbs not too different from those we have already let loose from the box marked To Deploy: from "heart-soothing" and "forthright speech" to "slander," "deceit," "discord," "fear," "strife," "lamentation," "consternation," and "rebellion" – both in the city itself and "on the land" (Wolkenstein and Kramer, 1983, 16–19). In the end, the river god accepts the gift of cityhood to humanity. Nonetheless – he rumbles from the distance – doing that hardly diminishes his fickle power over what is to come.

The story leaves human city dwellers with a future that we have shared across time, from the very origins of the Urban Condition to our Own Time. In that Condition, we exist as we are, devoid of divine wisdom in an urban present made of the urban past, in a space – our cities – where a lot is going on around us, with an expanded range of choices to take next, and with a wide array of limits on every one of those choices. Each morning, the tale of urban origins and urban futures begins anew, starring embodied and embedded beings who must envision a purpose, gather energy and power as our diverse situations permit, and from there deploy our power in projects of action that we deem most likely to give us the most headway possible toward our urban vision – modest or grand. The future that follows is exactly what the story of Inanna's riverboat delivery predicts, and exactly what a historical theory "by verb" confirms. All urban futures – past, present, and still to come – turn not on the moral superiority or inferiority of any space, or of any vision of a perfect space to come – but a gamble made up of *acts*.

If that seems like slim pickings to theorists and historians, that should signal us to accept the limits of our field of vision. In matters of urban futures, theorists, historians, and even goddesses can maybe learn the most from the professionals in the urban action business: *activists*. Like many urban studies scholars who either do or do not reveal this fact about themselves, I have been enormously fortunate to have learned almost everything I know about urban futures from some of the very best in the urban activism business. In 2005, I began teaching students about global urban history in the city of Buffalo, New York State, USA. That was a propitious time and place because, in the same year, Buffalo's West Side – economically beleaguered yet politically and culturally vibrant – encountered the prophetic genius of an alignment of activists who called themselves People United for Fair Housing – PUSH Buffalo for short.

PUSH Buffalo is a "situated" phenomenon, a "Community Based Organization" *par excellence*, devoted to the interests and visions of West Siders under the slogan "We Know What We Need Where We Live." Yet West Siders' urban knowledge comes from experiences that span the world and that cross every line of class, occupation, race, gender, sexuality, nation, and faith. Some PUSH leaders hail from the Seneca Nation of the native Haudenosaunee (Iroquois) Confederacy. Others are "born and raised" Buffalonians descended from families who migrated to the city in successive waves as it became an industrial and commercial powerhouse – from across Europe, from the post-slavery cotton-belt South, and from Puerto Rico. Many of their families remained on the West Side as the city's factories shuttered, as their neighbors moved to suburbs or the US "Sunbelt," and as Buffalo became a classic "shrinking city" – with over a one-quarter of its housing stock abandoned, in ruins, or carted away by city demolition crews as rubble. The West Side became a zone of depressed land prices and rents. That, however, also made it a magnet for refugee resettlement programs, and the neighborhood filled with new arrivals from Africa, Asia, the Caribbean, and Latin America. The West Side became a Global North city with many Global South character-istics, as Puerto Rican, Burmese, Karen, Somali Bantu, Congolese, Bangladeshi, Afghan, Syrian, Haitian, and Central American residents built organizations that reflected political and cultural conflicts in their own birth-places. Then, many brought their rich perspectives and organizing traditions to PUSH.

As community-based organizations go, PUSH was also particularly welcom-ing to professional architects, urban planners, theoreticians, and even historians. All of us added "expertise" where we could. But the experts that mattered most to PUSH's success hailed from the poorly paid, overworked, underappreciated, yet effervescent profession of community organizers. It was they who listened to residents' demands for clean, safe, affordable housing and energy, well-paid work, safe and productive recreation, fresh food, water, and air – and spun them into a series of virtuoso acts of alignment, catalysis, and amplified power. Organizers' insight is this: Visions of urban futures that are meaningful to urban majorities arise only from pounding urban pavements, knocking on doors, and holding thousands of conversations on porches. In PUSH's case, these encounters fueled member meetings, many held at an abandoned local library that PUSH purchased for a dollar from the city, but that also took place in immigrant association offices, a Boys and Girls Club, bars, cafes, and a disused city park that PUSH soon convinced City Hall to renovate.

Quickly, West Side residents and allies became a disruptive political force. "We are the Mighty, Mighty PUSH," crowds of new "movement leaders" chanted in street protests in front of abandoned homes and empty lots, at rallies in front of City Hall, in City Council chambers, in the lobbies of corporate headquarters of the city's gentrifying capitalist land development companies and its hydrocarbon-fracking gas utility, in the state capital of Albany, on the National Mall in Washington DC, and in hundreds of meetings with coalition partners from across the country and the world. The tricks of organizers' trade – "power mapping," movement "asset inventories," "issue-cutting," "issue-based coalitions," "target identification," "tension-raising," "public accountability sessions," "digital storming," moments of mobilization, and "inflection points for change" – are scarce in the terminology of urban theorists and urban historians. All represent fine-grained verbs that fit within nested conceptual boxes that make up "projects" of power amplification and deployment. Organizers have a different term for the best bets on the urban future they propose: "winnable campaigns."

In PUSH's case, each of these campaigns for an urban future began in a present moment and gained momentum as each day and week passed and as these campaigns themselves became historical phenomena. Along the way, they suffered setbacks, circled back "in-house" for readjustment, ducked and weaved in moments of improvisation, and shifted shape in ways that often mystified the local pantheon of power-accumulators, profiteers, misinformation peddlers, and arch-polluters – and often pulled "victories" out of the jaws of seemingly inevitable defeat. Victory celebrations, in turn, provided political fuel for new campaigns. *Acts*, meanwhile, produced new *activists* trained to amplify the power of their acts, fueled both by informed and courageous embodiment and city-energized embeddedness.

Acts of catalysis, recall, are not an inevitable "function" of concentration, diversification, and juxtaposition in thick space; any causal connection between space and power requires verification through historical evidence. The evidence of both catalysis and synergy on the West Side grew in volume – and, as such, it appropriately grew rapidly. Victories in campaigns that targeted a New York State agency designed to funnel tax liens on foreclosed West Side properties to Wall Street speculators allowed PUSH to bring increasing swaths of urban land under permanent community control – well before these same financial instruments helped trigger global capitalism's great crises of 2008. A similar campaign that successfully shamed the city's mayor for allowing abandoned city-owned properties to become dangers to neighbors added to PUSH's landholdings. Then, at a series of Community Planning Congresses, a growing throng of activists of many backgrounds inaugurated a 25-block "Green Development Zone" (GDZ). "Green" and "affordable" rhyme especially well when it comes to housing in Buffalo, because housing costs are driven as much by high home-heating bills as by rent. An alchemy developed between questions of justice and equity, energy conservation, and the production of renewable energy. On the West Side, cheap housing meant energy-efficient retrofits and cheap energy harvested on the West Side itself – both from Earth (geothermal) and Sun (photovoltaic panels). Within a few years, the working-class GDZ included over a hundred units of high-quality affordable housing, the region's most advanced net-zero and passive-solar domestic spaces, a geothermal system that heated some of the units, a program to insulate hundreds of other homes, dozens of parcels of land used for community gardens that showcased immigrant farming traditions and provided oases in a food desert, a youth center (in the library), and an arts center in an old laundromat run by a Burmese democracy activist. A PUSH-owned landscaping company introduced elements of urban sponginess, diverting rainwater into the Earth rather than into the combined sewer system that sent waste into the river and over Niagara Falls twenty miles to the North. Then, PUSH restored an entire school building, creating new offices, community spaces, a theater, a gym, a dozen more housing units for community elders, and festooned its rooftop with the region's first community solar array. A workforce training program meanwhile recruited West Siders into the energy efficiency and renewable energy businesses and will soon have its own multimillion dollar facility on a former toxic site on the West Side.

The scope of action expanded from there, as did the scope of the vision. National attention opened generous taps of foundation and government funding. Coalitions PUSH built won passage of the State's 2019 Community Leadership and Protection Act, a progressive policy to combat climate change by directing large funds through community organizations like PUSH that provided a model for national visions later partially enacted in federal legislation. The West Side, meanwhile, emerged as a crucial capital of the broader environmental justice movement, and PUSH committed itself to a shared grand future: a "Just Transition" from cities fueled by hydrocarbon to renewable energy controlled by the urban majority. That same movement calls on all of us to build the "Bigger We" required for the acts required to produce an Urban Planet that is truly Ours (Climate Justice Alliance, 2022; PUSH Buffalo, 2023).

"Humans," Hannah Arendt observed in one of her lectures on power, "appear to have a highly mysterious gift for making miracles. ... This gift is called action" (Arendt, 2018 [1960], 240). On an Urban Planet ruled by imperial states and capitalist corporations, threatened by a new virtual "town square" that could soon flood the most promising physical spaces of the urban *polis* with disinformation, and hurtling toward a series of "tipping points" that could transform Earth into an unbearable "Hothouse Planet," the miracles of action on the West Side – like many others elsewhere – may seem like little to go on. Indeed, as Earthopolis orbited through its *annus horribilis* of 2020, PUSH itself experienced forces of institutional overwhelm, internal factionalism, rollercoasters of euphoria and disappointment, and projects of brute opposition. Sometimes, "processes" such as "enduring empire," "capitalist urbanization," a culture of autocracy, and the creeping post-Holocenic predicaments of Our Time appear so relentless as to guarantee a real "end of history" too horrific for any of us to want to envision. A Just Transition, meanwhile, remains a long way off. It will of course require lots of state power and capital (hopefully more fairly and accountably accumulated) to get there, and when we get there, we will face many remaining existential predicaments. The Just Transition, meanwhile, is certainly not a vision of a "Small Planet." It will hardly slow the Great Acceleration of Our Urban Planet, nor the size of its photovoltaic or wind-turbine-covered urban hinterlands, nor its cities, nor its forelands of Action, Habitat, Impact, or Consequence to come. It will not slow the acceleration of the human population to above 11 billion, nor will it forestall the production of 50-to-80-million-person megacities by 2100. Nor will it stop new extra-human habitat disruption and loss, nor the pandemics and extinctions that result. It is a vision of a city that may behave somewhat more "mutualistically" with its surrounding natural ecosystems, but only somewhat; and it will certainly not restore the miraculous climate rhythms of the Holocene. Moreover, the future of even small miracles like those at PUSH depends on many possibly improbable things. First, the ongoing explosion of useful urban theory, history, and other types of urban research must be robust enough to roll back huge tides of disinformation to come. And far more of the world's governing institutions will need to make an expanding commitment to democracy. Yet even when PUSH activists resorted to "failing forward" – another great verb for urban theory – its activists woke once again each morning to produce new miracles of urban catalysis (*EP*, chapter 25).

As Arendt reminds us, miracles of space, time, power, and action, like those on the West Side of Buffalo, are also temporal phenomena with their own very "deep" history of claims on the urban future. "Action and beginning are essentially the same," she notes. "The whole frame of our real existence – the Earth, the organic life on it, the evolution of mankind out of animal species – rests on a chain of miracles. ... Every new beginning becomes a miracle the moment we look at it from the viewpoint of the process it has interrupted" (Arendt, 2018 [1960], 240–41).

If the concept *Our* Urban Planet is to be useful to theorists and historians, let its highest use be of the same use for all of us: As an inspiration to future interruptive acts of "Our" species' power, in all urban spaces, reiterated in time in the form of stubborn new beginnings each day, that produce a fuller future for all miracles of life – on both "Earthopolis" and Earth itself.

References

Angelo, Hillary and David Wachsmuth, 2014. "Urbanising Urban Political Ecology: A Critique of Methodological Cityism," *International Journal of Urban and Regional Research* 39: 16–27.

Arendt, Hannah, 1958. *The Human Condition* (Chicago: University of Chicago Press).

Arendt, Hannah, 2018 [1960] . "Freedom and Politics: A Lecture," in *Thinking Without Bannisters: Essays in Understanding, 1954–1975* (New York: Schocken Books)

Algaze, Guillermo, 2005. *The Uruk World System: The Dynamics of Expansion of Early Mesopotamian Civilization* (2nd ed., Chicago: Chicago University Press).

Brenner, Neil, 2017. "The *Problematique* of Critique," in Brenner, *Critique of Urbanization: Selected Essays*, Neil Brenner ed., (Gütersloh: Birkhäuser), pp. 16–24.

Brenner, Neil and Christian Schmid, 2015. "Toward a New Epistemology of the Urban?" *City* 19: 151–82.

Brooke, John L., 2014. *Climate Change and the Course of Global History: A Rough Journey* (Cambridge: Cambridge University Press).

Chakrabarty, Dipesh, 2021. *The Climate of History in a Planetary Age* (Chicago: University of Chicago Press).

Childe, Gordon Vere, 1950. "The Urban Revolution," *Town Planning Review* 21: 3–17.

Climate Justice Alliance, 2022. "How We Work," https://climatejusticealliance .org/how-we-work/. Accessed April 11, 2022.

Derrickson, Kate, 2018. "Masters of the Universe," *Environment and Planning D Society and Space* 36(3): 556–62.

Elis, Erle C. and Navin Ramankutty, 2008. "Putting People on the Map: Anthropogenic Biomes of the World," *Frontiers in Ecology and the Environment* 6: 439–47.

Elhacham, Emily, Liad Ben-Uri, Jonathan Grozovski, Yinon M. Bar-On, and Ron Milo, 2020. "Global Human Mass Exceeds All Living Biomass," *Nature* 588: 442–45.

Favereau, Marie, 2021. *The Horde: How the Mongols Changed the World* (Cambridge: Harvard University Press).

Fineman, Martha Albertson, 2024. "Introduction: Understanding Vulnerability," in *Law, Vulnerability, and the Responsive State: Beyond Equality and Liberty*,

Martha Albertson Fineman and Laura Spitz eds. (Abingdon: Routledge), pp. 1–10.

Future Cities Laboratory, 2023. "Extreme Territories of Urbanization," in *New Agendas Under Planetary Urbanisation [sic]*, https://planetaryurbanisation .ethz.ch/project/extreme-territories. Accessed November 7, 2023.

Glaser, Edward, 2011. *Triumph of the City: How Our Greatest Invention Makes Us Richer, Smarter, Greener, Healthier, and* Happier (New York: Penguin).

Global Urban History Project, 2020. "Theory of, for, and by Urban Historians," https://globalurbanhistory.org/content.aspx?page_id=22&club_id=803980& module_id=487348. Accessed August 28, 2023.

Graeber, David and David Wengrow, 2021. *The Dawn of Everything: A New History of Humanity* (New York: Farrar, Strauss, and Giroux).

Goonewardena, Kanishka, 2018. "Planetary Urbanization and Totality" *Environment and Planning D Society and Space* 36(3): 456–73.

Gordon, Avery F., 2008. *Ghostly Matters: Haunting and the Sociological Imagination* (2nd ed., Minneapolis: University of Minnesota Press).

Haff, Peter, 2014. "Technology as a Geological Phenomenon: Implications for Human Well Being," in *A Stratigraphical Basis for the Anthropocene*, C. N. Waters, J. Zalasiewicz, and Mark Williams eds. (London: Geological Society, Special Publications, 395), pp. 301–09.

Harris, Richard, 2021. *How Cities Matter* (Cambridge: Cambridge University Press, Cambridge Elements in Global Urban History).

Harvey, David, 1989. "The Urbanization of Capital," in *The Urban Experience*, David Harvey ed., (Baltimore: Johns Hopkins University Press), pp. 17–58.

Jacobs, Jane, 1961. *The Life and Death of Great American Cities* (New York: Vintage).

Jacobs, Jane, 1969. *The Economy of Cities* (New York: Vintage).

Kaika, Maria, Roger Keil, Tait Mandler and Yannis Tzaninis eds. 2023. *Turning Up the Heat: Urban Political Ecology for a Climate Emergency* (Manchester University Press).

Keil, Roger, 2018. "Extended Urbanization, 'Disjunct Fragments,' and Global Suburbanisms," *Environment and Planning D Society and Space* 36(3): 494–511.

Koselleck, Reinhard, 2018. *Sediments of Time: On Possible Histories*, trans. and eds. Sean Franzel and Stefan-Ludwig Hoffmann (Palo Alto: Stanford University Press).

Kostof, Spiro, 1991. *The City Shaped: Urban Patterns and Meanings through History* (New York: Little Brown).

Lefebvre, Henri, 1968 [1971]. *La vie quotidienne dans le monde moderne*, trans. Sacha Rabinovitch (Allen Lane: The Penguin Press).

Lefebvre, Henri, 1974 [1991]. *The Production of Space*, trans. Donald Nicholson-Smith (Malden: Blackwell).

Lefebvre, Henri, 1970 [2003]. *The Urban Revolution*, trans. Robert Bonnono. (Minneapolis: University of Minnesota Press)

Lewis, Simon L. and Mark Maslin, 2018. *The Human Planet: How We Created the Anthropocene* (New Haven: Yale University Press).

Liverani, Mario, 1998. *Uruk: The First City* (Sheffield: Equinox).

McIntosh, Roderick J., 2006. *Ancient Middle Niger: Urbanism and the Self-Organizing Landscape* (Cambridge: Cambridge University Press).

Moore, Jason W., 2017. "The Capitalocene, Part I: On the Nature and Origins of Our Ecological Crisis," *The Journal of Peasant Studies* 44: 594–630.

Moore, Jerry D., 2012. *The Prehistory of Home* (Berkeley: University of California Press).

Nightingale, Carl, 2012. *Segregation: A Global History of Divided Cities* (Chicago: University of Chicago Press).

Nightingale, Carl, 2015. "The Seven C's: Reflections on Writing a Global History of Urban Segregation," in *Cities beyond Borders: Comparative and Transnational Approaches to Urban History*, Nicholas Kenney and Rebecca Madgin eds. (Farnham: Ashgate), pp. 27–42.

Nightingale, Carl, 2022. *Earthopolis: A Biography of Our Urban Planet* (Cambridge: Cambridge University Press).

Ong, Aihwa, 2012. "Worlding Cities or the Art of Being Global," in *Worlding Cities: Asian Experiments and the Art of Being Global*, Ananya Roy and Aihwa Ong eds. (Chichester: Wiley Blackwell),

PUSH Buffalo, 2023. PUSH Buffalo website at PUSHBuffalo.org. Accessed November 1, 2023.

Roy, Ananya, 2015. "What is Critical about Critical Urban Theory," *Urban Geography* 37(6): 1–14.

Ruddiman, William F., 2014. *Earth Transformed* (New York: Freeman).

Schayegh, Cyrus, 2017. "Transpatialization: A New Heuristic Model to Think about Modern Cities," *Global Urban History* blog, December 14, at globalurbanhistory.com. Accessed August 29, 2023.

Schmid, Christian, 2018. "Journeys in Planetary Urbanization: Decentering Perspectives on the Urban," *Environment and Planning D Society and Space* 36(3): 591–610.

Sennett, Richard, 1977. *Fall of Public Man* (New York: Knopf).

Shryock, Andrew and Daniel Lord Smail, 2011. *Deep History: The Architecture of Past and Present* (Berkeley: University of California Press).

Soja, Edward, 2000. *Postmetropolis: Critical Studies of Cities and Regions* (Oxford: Blackwell).

Simone, AbdouMaliq, 2022. "Conclusion: Turbulent Urbanities," *Antipode*, https://antipodeonline.org/wp-content/uploads/2023/03/AbdouMaliq-Simone_conclusion.pdf. Accessed August 28, 2023.

Smith, Michael E., 2019. "Energized Crowding and the Generative Role of Settlement Aggregation and Scaling," in *Coming Together: Comparative Approaches to Population Aggregation and Early Urbanization*, Attila Gyucha ed. (Albany: State University of New York Press), pp. 37–58.

Stoler, Ann Laura, 2016. *Duress: Imperial Durabilities in Our Times* (Durham: Duke University Press,).

Tzaninis, Yannis, Tait Mandler, Roger Keil and Marria Kaika, 2023. "Introduction: Political Ecology for a Climate Emergency," in *Turning Up the Heat: Urban Political Ecology for a Climate Emergency*, Maria Kaika, Roger Keil, Tait Mandler, and Yannis Tzaninis. eds. (Manchester University Press), pp. 1–34.

Thomas, Julia Adeney, Mark Williams, and Jan Zalasiewicz, 2020. *The Anthropocene: A Multidisciplinary Approach* (Cambridge: Polity Press).

Thomas, Julia Adeney, 2022. *Altered Earth: Getting the Anthropocene Right* (Cambridge: Cambridge University Press).

Tilly, Charles, 1996. "What Good Is Urban History?" *Journal of Urban History* 22: 702–719.

Vergès, Françoise, 2017. "Racial Capitalocene," in *Futures of Black Radicalism*, Gaye Theresa Johnson and Alex Lubin eds. (New York: Verso), pp. 72–82.

Wallerstein, Emanuel, 1974. *The Modern World-System, Vol. I: Capitalist Agriculture and the Origins of the European World-Economy in the Sixteenth Century* (New York: Academic Press).

Weaver, Warren, 1947. "Science and Complexity," *American Scientist* 36: 536–44.

Whitehead, Colson, 2021. *Harlem Shuffle* (New York: Doubleday).

Wirth, Louis, 1938. "Urbanism as a Way of Life," *American Sociological Review* 44: 1–24.

Wolkenstein, Diane and Samuel Noah Kramer, 1983. *Inanna, Queen of Heaven and Earth: Her Stories and Hymns from Sumer* (New York: Harper and Row).

Yusoff, Katheryn, 2019. *A Billion Black Anthropocenes* (Minneapolis: University of Minnesota Press).

Zalasiewicz, Jan and Mark Williams, 2012. *The Goldilocks Planet: The Four-Billion-Year Story of Earth's Climate* (Oxford: Oxford University Press).

Acknowledgements

I dedicate this Element to the only proper theorist in my house, the one I am married to: Martha T. McCluskey. The courage she has displayed deploying idea-power within the far-more contentious world of Law and Political Economy encouraged me to try my own hand with Our Urban Planet. Among other things, she introduced me to the work of her mentor and collaborator Martha Albertson Fineman, whose pioneering explorations of human vulnerability through our embodiment and embeddedness helped ground my readings of "deep history", and to the work of Hannah Arendt, whose reading of human power I think is extremely useful to urban historians.

The ideas in this Element emerged amidst stimulating conversations within my intellectual home base, the Global Urban History Project, and especially in frequent conversations with Rosemary Wakeman about theory and temporality, Alexia Yates about energy, power, real estate, and capitalism; Kenny Cupers, Wangui Kimari, and Anwesha Ghosh about Global South Urbanism, Cyrus Schayegh about empire and multiscalar change, and Greet De Block about theory and history. I have also benefitted tremendously from an overlapping conversation on Cities and the Anthropocene led by Toby Lincoln, Debjani Bhattacharyya, Mark Williams, Jan Zalasiewicz, Julia Adeney Thomas, Sam Grinsell, and Vyta Pivo. Over the past few years, these two core groups invited many other luminaries from both history and theory to our table, many of whom are cited in these pages, and all of whom have shared exquisite insight. Long intellectual friendships with Mariana Dantas, Nancy Kwak, Emma Hart, Kristin Stapleton, Hou Li, and recent conversations with Sheetal Chhabria and Abosede George all influenced this text. My great admiration and gratitude to the tireless trio of editors who have brought the Cambridge Elements in Global Urban History into such resplendent life: Michael Goebel, Tracy Neumann, and, my own editor, Joseph Ben Prestel, all of whom have given me many opportunities to rehearse and refine these ideas in conversation. Thanks also to the anonymous scholars who reviewed a much flimsier first draft of this work and urged me to take it to another level.

In my text, I have already acknowledged the visionaries I have been so lucky to intersect with in the beloved *polis* of Buffalo, New York: the visionary activists and fellow supporters of People United for Sustainable Housing, PUSH Buffalo. Among them are the truest miracle makers I know of: Aaron Bartley, Rahwa Ghirmatzion, Dawn Wells-Clyburn, Sam Magavern, Anna Falicov, Kevin Connor, Sarah Gordon, Clark Gocker, and Jim Anderson.

To all of you and to many others: I can't tell you how lucky I feel that we all dwell together on Earthopolis in the early twenty-first century– to gather scraps of power still available on Our Urban Planet, and to concoct projects to bend Our Volatile Time in surprising ways. . . . I am sure that all these projects will be a treat for global urban historians to discover in the archives of the future.

Cambridge Elements ☰

Global Urban History

Printed in the United States
by Baker & Taylor Publisher Services